THE JOURNEY INWARD

Miguel, the Mexican-Indian Shaman with whom author Dr. Susan Gregg studied, told her being free means being able to have whatever you want whenever you want it. But in order to achieve this personal freedom, you must take a journey that will completely transform the way you experience life and reality.

Dance of Power is the story of Dr. Gregg's journey into the world of shamanism, where she discovered a world view completely different from her former, static perception of life.

If you have ever questioned the way you have been taught to view the universe, now you can journey along the path of the Nagual, and take a quantum leap along the path toward personal freedom. Did you know that you are already a perfect being? You are already free—you have just forgotten it. *Dance of Power* will help you remember your birthright as a happy, spiritual being, and will help you find the truth of who you are.

Join Dr. Gregg as she re-lives her personal experiences: her first meeting and studies with Miguel, her travel to other realms (without the use of drugs), and her subsequent initiations into the life of a "warrior." Learn from her victory over her internal struggles: overcoming the fear of change; abandoning one's sense of self-importance in order to gain personal power; and winning the ultimate battle of spirit over mind—achieving a sense of oneness with life and with death.

After you have achieved your personal freedom, the spiritual "you" will be in charge...that's what it means to follow the path of the Nagual, and become totally responsible for your own reality. After you embark upon this solitary, spiritual journey, your world will never be the same.

ABOUT THE AUTHOR

Dr. Susan Gregg was born and raised in New York City. She graduated in 1972 from the University of Vermont with a BA in Mathematics. At this time she also began to explore metaphysics, including transcendental meditation.

After moving to California in the 1980s, Susan met a Mexican Nagual or Shaman and became his apprentice. When she finished her apprenticeship, the Nagual told her to go out and teach in her own manner.

In 1989 Susan received her Doctorate in Clinical Hypnotherapy. She also became a Reverend in the Universal Church of the Master in Santa Clara, California. Susan now lives in Hawaii with her springer spaniel. She is in private practice assisting people in transforming their lives. She lives happily by the beach in a sleepy town, enjoying life on a daily basis.

TO WRITE TO THE AUTHOR

If you wish to contact the author or would like more information about this book, please write to the author in care of Llewellyn Worldwide and we will forward your request. Both the author and publisher enjoy hearing from you and learning of your enjoyment of this book and how it has helped you. Llewellyn Worldwide cannot guarantee that every letter written to the author will be answered, but all will be forwarded. Please write to:

DR. SUSAN GREGG
c/o LLEWELLYN WORLDWIDE
P.O. Box 64383, dept. L247-0
St. Paul, Minnesota 55164-0383, U.S.A.

Please enclose a self-addressed, stamped envelope for reply, or $1.00 to cover costs. If outside the U.S.A. enclose international postal reply coupon.

Dance

of

Power

A *Shamanic* *Journey*

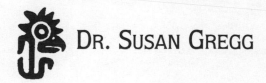 Dr. Susan Gregg

1997
Llewellyn Publications
St. Paul, Minnesota 55164-0383, U.S.A.

FIRST EDITION
Fourth Printing, 1997

Cover painting: LISSANNE LAKE
Interior illustrations: ALEXANDRA LUMEN
Book design and layout: MICHELLE DAHN

Library of Congress Cataloging-in-Publication Data
Gregg, Susan
    Dance of power : a shamanic journey / Susan Gregg
        p.   cm.
    ISBN 0-87542-247-0
    1. Shamanism. 2. Gregg, Susan. 3. Shamans--United States
--Biography. I. Title.
BF1611.G   1993
291.1'4--dc20   93-30704
                                                           CIP

Llewellyn Publications
A Division of Llewellyn Worldwide, Ltd.
P.O. Box 64383, St. Paul, MN 55164-0383

✪ Printed on recycled paper

DEDICATION

This book is dedicated to that sacred place
within each of us that is always at peace.

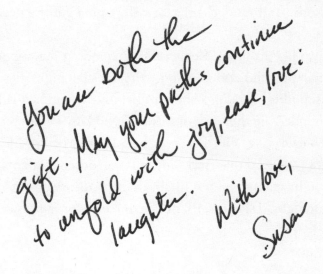

You are both the gift. May your paths continue to unfold with joy, ease, love & laughter.

With love,
Susan

ACKNOWLEDGEMENTS

I would like to thank all my teachers especially Jeanne Lang for her gentleness and love. I would like to thank the people at Llewellyn. Nancy, thanks for seeing this book lurking within my first book.

G. Tony Bruce, thank you for being my mentor and a friend. Your encouragement made this book possible and so did your computer lessons. And June, thanks for helping me get the new computer.

I would also like to thank Rebecca for reminding me about the rules of grammar and composition...the Tuesday night class for its loving support...my dog Ashtar for her loyalty and her wet kisses that reminded me there was a world beyond my computer.

Thanks to everyone who has ever been a part of my life. Miguel, Sarita, Leslie, Francisco, and all the other students, thank you, you have touched my life in so many different ways. And last but not least, I want to thank the universe for rainbows.

◆ ◆

TABLE OF CONTENTS

I discuss how I met Miguel and began my studies with him.

The most frightening part of my studies was my journey through the tunnel. I talk about the beginning of that journey as well as my battle with inorganic beings.

Miguel begins a series of classes to teach his basic philosophy. It is my first opportunity to understand the new way in which I was experiencing my world.

In this chapter the nature of the universe, the way I was taught to view it in the past, and how I view it now are discussed. I briefly explain the nature of energy and how we create our reality.

This chapter covers our security point, or comfort zone, and explains how defending it decreases our ability to change. I discuss the nature of change and how we can make change easier and less threatening.

Before I was able to move up to the next stage in my training as an apprentice, I was required to do open eye meditations in front of a mirror. During the process I learned how to sort out emotions left over from my childhood and past lives. In this chapter I discuss some of my experiences and share some of the insights.

After I completed each phase of my studies there was an initiation or ceremony in which I was given permission to "handle" more power. The Water Initiation was a beautiful ceremony in which Miguel told us we were changed spiritually and physically. I talk about the ceremony as well as how it affected my personal life.

I discuss how habits and routines keep us stuck in our old way of being in the world. I will talk about some of the experiences I had as I began to lead a life that was moving towards having personal freedom. Miguel defined freedom as the ability to be placed anywhere on the earth and be able to flourish.

In our world there are many facts we can understand. In the universe there is much that we can never understand. Knowing the difference allows us to operate within the sphere of things that we can control. The "old ones" wasted a great deal of energy trying to understand the unknowable. By defining the unknowable, we are better able to know our limits. I talk about these limits, as well as give some history on the "old ones."

There are two ways to access information on the ethereal level. The way of dreamers and/or stalkers. In this chapter I explore both paths.

Magic and power are how we create our reality. They are both reflections of each other. I discuss their nature as well as some of the pitfalls of dabbling in magic and misusing power.

I provide a description of the ceremony, its ramifications, and its effect on me as well as some of the other apprentices.

Personal power and personal importance are inversely proportional. The more you have of one, the less you have of the other. In order to succeed on this path I had to build my personal power and get rid of my sense of personal importance. In this chapter I elaborate on this process.

One of the most important aspects of this path is to gain power
and use it wisely. I talk about the process of stalking or gaining
power. I explore some of the ways power can be used. I discuss
the power of the spoken word and the use of invocations.

I describe the ceremony in which Miguel made me a medicine
woman or woman of power. I also touch briefly on the ending of
our formal studies together.

I talk about my own apprentices and the completion of my formal studies with Miguel

I reflect on my early years and what lead me to be a seeker of
the truth.

I share my dreams about creating heaven on earth.

This section gives definitions of key phrases found in the text.

INTRODUCTION

*We see things not as they are,
but as we are.*

Late March in Vermont is a difficult month. By then winter has lasted a few months too long. The snow is still on the ground, but it is tired looking, all gray and gritty. Your body screams for spring and warmth.

After living there for many years, I finally decided I was tired of being cold. It was time to move. Years before a psychic had told me I'd be leaving Vermont, and I had thought she was crazy. Now I realized she wasn't crazy after all. I decided to move to southern California, although I'd never been there before.

One gray, cold day soon after making that decision, I found myself sitting in a back room of a bookstore listening to a woman channel an entity who called himself the Chief, a very gentle soul who talked about our connection to nature and the earth.

On this March day, he talked to me about the long journey I would take. A journey in which I would find my soul. He told me about the magic of the desert and said that there was a great, wise teacher waiting for me. He went on to talk about the colorful cast of characters I would meet and about the courage it would take to walk through the valley of shadows.

Little did I know that day how right he was. As I look back, everything he said was true. But that day I had no idea what was in store for me. All I felt was nervous anticipation.

I certainly never expected to be studying with a Nagual. During the seventies, a friend of mine and I had read all the Carlos Castaneda books about Don Juan. Reading those books I had felt more fear than curiosity. I didn't at all feel drawn to experience that kind of testing. My friend had actually gone to Mexico in search of a teacher but came back empty handed and disappointed. Imagine my surprise when, years later, I found myself studying with a Nagual.

A Nagual is a Mexican-Indian Shaman, or healer, whose traditions go back to the Toltec and Aztec Indians. Since the time of the Spanish conquistadors, their existence has been shadowy and secret. They are wizards of sorts who can perform amazing feats. Some can change forms, others can create doubles, and most are healers.

Traditionally a Nagual has seven apprentices who comprise a band or group. That band is often referred to as a ring of fire or ring of power. If they could be viewed as energy, these rings look like a series of concentric circles stretching back into history.

When Miguel, the Nagual I studied with, took his training, he had to promise to pass the knowledge on to seven other people. I ended up being the one of the seven in his ring of fire. His teacher did not believe in the use of drugs. He said drugs limited a warrior's strength. He believed it was better to know how to travel to the other realms without depending on drugs.

During the time I studied with Miguel, I found out that the path of the Nagual is a way of life. Once you embark on it, the world never seems the same. Reality becomes illusion. It is a path on which you strive to build your personal power. The pay-backs for the misuse of that power are immense. To become an apprentice you need a sense of dedication. The path is an arduous one that takes you through various stages.

The first stage is that of a student. The only requirements for being a student are curiosity and imagination. Next the apprentice begins to make a bid for power. At this important stage the student becomes a hunter and begins to "stalk" power. The skills you gain as a hunter are the foundation for the rest of the studies. They teach you how to learn in the various realities. In order to be a hunter, you have to have awareness, patience, perseverance, and careful observation of routines. Very few people complete this phase of the training.

The final stage of the process is to become a warrior. To be a warrior you have to be alert, in control of your emotions, and ready to act. Then you have to choose the right moment to act. You also need an opponent. Impure intentions are one of the opponents. Many people lose their focus at this point and get caught up in the phenomenon of using their new-found power to control and manipulate others.

Traditionally one of the warrior's opponents is death. The strongest and most dangerous is the warrior's ego. As the warrior

handles more power, it is easy to misuse it and hurt him or herself and others. The Naguals of the past had not "caught the
energy" properly and continued to fear death. They tried to find
ways to preserve their personal power after their death. They
had perceived the universe as a large eagle that ate your spirit as
you died. I believe they misinterpreted their visions of the oneness of the universe.

I learned to interpret the energy myself. I eventually experienced a sense of oneness at death rather than oblivion. The
spirit lives on. The entire process is a battle to see who will be in
charge of your life, the spiritual being or the mind.

The mind is incredibly powerful. Our minds believe the
struggle is a matter of their survival, so they make the process of
achieving freedom as hard as possible. Our minds would rather
see us dead than free. My mind knew that the goal of my studies was my personal freedom. Once I achieved my freedom, my
spiritual self would be in charge, and my mind would no longer
be calling the shots.

I finally learned that the ultimate goal is the freedom to
choose moment by moment what you want to experience. The
quest is about personal freedom. Miguel once told me that if I
was truly free, he could drop me off any place on this planet
without money or knowing the language and I would flourish.

Achieving freedom continues to be an amazing journey. I am
still processing some of the information I received. Each time I
teach the concepts, they make more sense.

For much of this journey there are no words. Often the best
I can do is share how I felt at the time.

I hope you enjoy the journey.

THE DREAM

The wind was hot and gritty as it blew over the desert. Little dust clouds rose up here and there, reminding anyone who cared enough to notice of the power of the wind. As it passed through the canyons, it howled and picked up speed until it virtually roared over the cliffs.

The old woman stood at the edge of the cliff looking down at the desert. "How many years have I been here waiting?" she mused. The wind blew through her and her sigh combined with the wind's wailing.

That night as the sun set, she saw a campfire off in the distance. As the sky lost its last traces of crimson she approached the camp site. Much to her relief, a lone woman sat by the fire. At last thought the old woman, tonight I can tell my last story so I can leave and join my ancestors.

She sat in the shadows for a time and observed the other woman. As the old woman looked into her dark eyes, she could see a brave spirit. She knew she was looking upon a woman of power. The woman at the campfire appeared deep in thought and was chanting quietly. Her voice was haunting and otherworldly. As the wind became more gentle, the old woman could hear little bits of her song. She was talking to the spirits of this land and asking for a vision. The old woman knew her waiting was over. As she stepped into the light, the woman turned and greeted her.

"Grandmother I have been waiting for you. Please come and join me by the fire. The night is dark. This is a night of power and I welcome you with all my heart."

The old woman sat down and reached out her hand. It was nice to be greeted with love instead of fear for a change.

"Listen my child, I have watched and waited for one like you. It is time for me to tell my story one last time. It saddens me that so many have forgotten."

The woman offered the old woman some tea, but she shook her head and continued speaking. "You are a special being. The Great Spirit created you and there is no other like you. In the whole universe you are the only one exactly like you. You really are a reflection of the Great Spirit's love. You have come here to remember who you are, then remind others of who they are. You, too, are a great storyteller. You must share your love and knowledge with anyone who will listen with an open heart."

"You have come here to remember that you are love and the only thing that is real is love. Everything else is an illusion. This physical world is so beautiful and sensual that it is easy to lose your way."

"The seasons come and go and we mourn the loss of our youth. We begin to believe that we are a body. We forget our divinity. We wander through life unfulfilled and empty. We try to fill that emptiness with the pleasures of this world and forget our way home. We lose sight of the truth and begin to believe only in the illusion. We forget we are one with the Great Spirit. We forget how precious each person is; we actually hurt one another." The old woman's eyes filled with tears at the thought of people hurting people.

"We have forgotten that our real strength lies in our gentleness. Who has ever won a war? Everyone loses unless they are coming from the realm of love. Only love is real.

"Learn to listen to your heart little one, learn to walk and live in love. Let love be the answer to all your questions. Never listen to the voice of judgement or anger. Listen only to the gentle whisperings of love."

The old woman talked on for hours about the history of the world and its people. She talked of the ways of power and the wisdom of the heart. She talked until she could talk no more. When she was finished, the old woman gratefully took the cup of tea the young woman offered.

As the old woman got up to leave she said, "Listen for my stories in the whispers of the wind. Listen to the truth in the gurgling of a mountain brook. Nature remembers the truth. Be still and listen. Listen to your heart's guidance and you will always be in the right place to gain knowledge."

"Walk always in love and step lightly upon the mother. You are safe my little one. You are always held lovingly in the heart of the universe."

The woman awoke from her dream. She looked frantically around for the old woman, but found no one. She warmed her hands over the fire and tried to remember her dream. The only thing she could recall was something about the wind. At that moment the wind came up and she thought she heard a melodic voice. And she listened.

◆◆◆◆◆◆◆◆◆◆◆◆◆ **1** ◆◆◆◆◆◆◆◆◆◆◆◆◆

THE MEETING

Even the longest journey
begins with the first step.

The blue eye inside the large pyramid stared out at me as I nervously approached the building. I was outside the temple of Sister Sarita, a Mexican healer who performed psychic surgery and was well-known for her miraculous cures.

I paced back and forth, struck by the contrast between the pyramid on one side of the door and the large, colorful fruits painted on the other side. The building, a converted laundromat, was in the barrio of a southern California city.

I felt out of place, like I was in a separate reality, having just moved to California from rural Vermont. The large, vibrant paintings of Aztec warriors and Mexican laborers on the huge freeway columns at the entrance to the barrio had already made me realize that I was about to enter a world that was totally unfamiliar to me.

Even though I felt excited, my fear would have driven me away except for the fact that I totally trusted Mary, the woman I was waiting for. I had only met her a few weeks before when I had accidentally attended the "wrong" spiritualist church.

Before I left Vermont, a friend had given me the address and time of services for a spiritualist church she knew about. Three days after I arrived in California I was scanning the newspaper when I saw Mary's spiritualist church listed at the same address. Although the time of service was different, I assumed it was the same church my friend had recommended. I didn't find out until months later that there were two spiritualist churches that had services at different times at the same address.

The minute I walked into that church I felt welcomed and totally at home. Mary, a woman in her 70s with a lined face, immediately greeted me with open arms. She gave me a huge hug and acted as if she had been waiting for me to come home again. I felt like I had known her all my life. Perhaps I had.

I was basically a shy person then, but Mary immediately introduced me to the other members of the church. Much to my amazement, she began telling everyone I was a great healer and a teacher. I just chalked that comment up to her being a "Californian." Everyone had warned me about the weirdos I would meet in California.

About a week after we had met, Mary told me there was a place she wanted to take me, Sister Sarita's temple. Now I was anxiously waiting for Mary to arrive and accompany me on this new adventure.

When she finally arrived, we walked through the entryway, which reminded me of my grandmother's apartment in

Queens. It even smelled the same. Above the door a transom stood ajar. The door led into a dark hallway, just like my grandmother's apartment.

As my eyes adjusted to the darkness, I noticed a window at the end of the hallway. The window looked into a closet filled with white coats. I wondered what the coats were for.

The main room was carpeted with an old, stained green shag rug. A bare bulb burned in the center of the ceiling. I concentrated on the wobbly, dusty ceiling fan in an attempt to calm my nerves.

Mary and I sat down on two of the twenty, metal folding chairs that encircled the room. People sat in the other chairs, talking loudly in Spanish. Mary mingled, greeting her friends. I felt very disconnected because I didn't understand the language.

I began to notice the rest of the temple. At the front of the room stood an altar, framed by dusty and faded gold velvet curtains. Behind the altar was a painting of a pyramid with a blue eye in the clouds. Shafts of light streamed outward from the pyramid, and a shadow of a cross loomed over the clouds. On the altar were a variety of old glass jars filled with faded gladiolus and yellow and gold mums.

In a corner, by the altar, sat a short, fat woman with a radiant smile. People congregated around her, and she seemed to be blessing them. After a time I realized this was Sister Sarita.

Mary came back to my seat and led me over to Sister Sarita, who stood up and gave me a big hug. I again felt very welcomed. She spoke to me rapidly in Spanish. Unfortunately I didn't understand a word, but intuitively I knew I had a connection with this woman.

We returned to our seats and Sister Sarita began speaking. Fortunately someone translated for me. Sarita was blessing the people and preparing her students to do healings. She sat down and went into trance, as did other people in the room.

Suddenly people began moving around and muttering while in a trance. By now the hallway was filled with families from the barrio. I later learned that on this particular night of the week, Sarita and her band performed free healing for people from the barrio.

Two men in white jackets guided people to the various healers. I'm sure my eyes were the size of saucers by then. One woman next to me began to suck on a woman's leg and spit out blood clots. I wanted to run out screaming. Instead I sat there and watched with fascination and horror.

A short, dark man approached me. His eyes really caught my attention. They were very, very dark—almost black. I seemed to be drawn into them. They looked almost like a cat's eyes. His presence was very powerful. He felt like a walking contradiction. He was threatening and comforting at the same time. And he seemed ageless.

He motioned to me. I had no idea what he wanted me to do. Then I realized he wanted me to perform a healing on him. He smiled and motioned for me to make sweeping motions around his body. So I did. He smiled again. His smile reminded me of the Cheshire Cat in *Alice in Wonderland*. It seemed to linger on his lips. It was part mystery, part humor, and very challenging.

I would not normally have participated in this ritual. I would have felt too foolish to try something new in front of strangers. But something about this man compelled me to follow his lead.

After I was finished, a woman who spoke English came over and translated for this mysterious man. She said that he wanted me to join his class on Saturday night. I said I'd be there. As he turned and smiled at me, he looked like a cat that had just swallowed the canary.

I later learned that he was Sister Sarita's youngest son, Miguel, a Nagual or Mexican shaman. His father and his father's father had been Naguals. Sarita's father had always said Miguel would follow the family's tradition, but he became a medical doctor instead. Then, while he was in the interior of Mexico finishing up his medical training, he began to study with a Nagual. Eventually he gave up a lucrative medical practice to follow his spiritual path.

All day the following Saturday I had a sense of nervous anticipation about the class that evening. As I entered the temple there was a chill in the air. I wasn't looking forward to seeing people sucking blood clots again.

There was a much smaller group of people that night, about eight, and some of them were speaking English. They were joking and talking as if they knew one another very well. When Miguel spotted me, he came over and gave me a large hug and welcomed me warmly.

Sarita cleared her throat. Everyone took a seat and class began. She was talking about the history of the five humanities and the energies of the human egg. These concepts were totally foreign to me so none of it made any sense. I also found it confusing listening to her and a translator simultaneously.

After the other students had asked their questions, we took a short break. After the break, Miguel and Sarita guided the students into specific locations for the meditation. In the center of the circle, they formed a human triangle. At the center of the triangle, they placed a huge, light brown crystal cluster.

The meditation began. Miguel and Sarita circulated around the room. As they stood in front of the students, their hands hovered over various points in the body. They would stand there making circular movements over certain areas of their bodies. At times they would pull upwards and away as if they were removing something. I later learned that they were working on people's power points. In effect they were acting as channels or conduits for energy they had accessed from the universe. As they did this, they were able to assist the person in releasing blockages from their body and aura.

When my time arrived, I felt like I was going to be blasted into another universe. The heat coming from their hands was amazing, and I felt like I was on fire. At first I found myself resisting the experience, but after a few minutes I allowed myself to open up. I could feel emotions and thoughts rising up to the surface. My mind began to swirl around, and I felt like my body was spinning. I later realized that my consciousness was trying to leave my body.

At the end of the meditation, everyone formed a circle and held hands. Miguel motioned for me to sit in the center of the circle. I thought I felt jealousy coming from some of the other students. The group chanted OM seven times. The room resonated with energy. As I look back, I realize that this was my initiation as Miguel's seventh apprentice.

At first I attended classes on Saturday evenings. The other apprentices had been studying with him for varying lengths of time. As the newcomer I felt uncomfortable asking questions. Everyone else seemed to know what was going on.

Luckily one of the other students translated. Sarita also often sat in and taught the classes. After a time I found myself listening more to her than to her translator. At some level I seemed to sense or understand what she was saying.

Over the holidays classes stopped meeting and I found myself studying alone with Miguel. Although he was beginning to learn English, there was a real language barrier. He could communicate directions for exercises, but was unable or unwilling to talk about abstracts. I now realize what a blessing that was. The biggest handicap I've had in my studies has been my mind. I have a quick mind that loves to talk to me. My mind always wants a rational explanation, so it is difficult to go beyond this reality. This path is not about rational explanations; it is about seeing the world in a totally different way.

With Miguel most of my early lessons were completely experiential. There were often no words to explain them. Miguel told me that I was learning on the ethereal level. He said it might take years for me to consciously remember the information. But he assured me the information would be there when I needed it. He said the fastest way to recall it was to teach. He said the students actually push the teacher to grow.

It took me years to fully understand what he meant by gaining information on the ethereal level. He was literally teaching my spirit lessons and by-passing my conscious mind. As I cleared out the emotional garbage from my past, it became easier to access that knowledge. Remarkably I did find that the information was always available to me whenever I needed it.

Miguel was one of the most peaceful people I ever met. In all the years I studied with him, I never saw him truly upset. Just being in his presence I felt a sense of safety, a feeling of unconditional love. Unless he had "that smile." When he smiled in a certain way, I learned I was about to embark on an adventure I might have preferred to avoid. Whenever I was in his presence, I also felt like I was in a separate reality. I found myself drawn to spend more and more time with him.

I worked from six o'clock in the morning until noon, so I often spent my afternoons with Miguel. We frequently went to a park near the beach or worked in the temple.

Southern California may be sunny, but it is not warm. The temple had no heat, so when we worked in there it was amazingly damp, cold, and clammy. Some afternoons he would give me a massage. The only similarity to a traditional massage was that the body was rubbed. He would work very deeply in my energy field. At times I would suddenly experience intense emotions or feel like the world had shifted somehow. At times it actually felt like I had been crooked in my body, and as Miguel worked I could feel myself straightening out.

After the massage we would do what he called a flying meditation. I would lie on the floor of the temple face down with my head in his lap. He placed a hand on either side of my head, and I went into a deep meditation. After a time he would push on my power points and I would leave my body. Power points are similar to the chakras. They are areas in the body that interface with our various energy bodies or emotional systems. In a sense they are switching stations. Depending on how and where Miguel pushed, I would be propelled into an altered state of consciousness. When Miguel would push my power points I could feel myself slowly peeling up out of my body usually feet first. Sometimes it felt like I was pure consciousness flying through space. At other times I felt intense surges of emotions flowing uncontrollably through my body. My mind would generally be standing off to the side severely critiquing my experience. When I returned after what seemed like minutes, my body would be all cramped up because I had been gone for so long.

Often we would go for walks along the beach. When he took me outside, he would have me put my "attention" on objects in nature. He told me to sense what I felt there. I realized later that he was trying to assist me in seeing the doors to other realities. At first I was a very slow, but persistent, student. I was unable to "see" anything beyond the tree or the ripples on the ocean.

One day Miguel had me sit in a tree and stare at the shadows on the ocean. After a time I felt as if I were being pulled out of myself and into an energy field of some sort. Miguel warned me not to lose myself, but to continue to focus my attention on the shadows in the water. I could feel a crack in my world—a door to another universe. It was an energy level or a reality without physical form as we know it, but it was just as real, if not more real than our universe.

The beings there had just as hard a time "seeing" our universe as I did theirs. I found myself standing at the edge of a long, dark corridor. I no longer had a body. I was pure consciousness. At the end of the hallway I could see several luminescent beings. They were rather large, but not at all frightening. They were aware of my presence and seemed to be beckoning me to enter their world. I heard Miguel off in the distance warning me not to lose myself. I sensed that these beings were very loving and kind. I sensed absolutely no hostility or judgements of any sort. I was intrigued and wanted to step out of the corridor and into their universe. I hesitated for an instant, uncertain whether I should proceed or not, and I found myself instantly being pulled back into my world. On that pure energy level thoughts were manifested instantly, there was no time lag.

Eventually I found that each universe seemed to have an entry fee. I found that my intention or my reason for being there influenced my experience. For example, if I went there to learn, I gathered information. When I had a sense of purpose I would come back with the necessary knowledge. But if I was unclear about why I was there, I got fuzzy information. I would come back feeling confused and disoriented.

I was never sure what sort of energies I would encounter in these realms. Each "world" had its own rules and operating instructions. Some of the worlds were joyful and light, while others were absolutely terrifying. I felt like I was on an emotional roller coaster. At times I felt like I was, as Miguel put it, "coming crazy." He often warned me that insanity was a real possibility if I went too fast.

Fear became an intimate companion as I continued to study with Miguel. My mind had no reference point for what was going on. Our society has no way to explain shamans or journeys into the ethereal or the inorganic beings that were beginning to haunt me. They just weren't part of my upbringing. The scary monsters under the bed were familiar, but those were kids' things.

One day we were sitting on the sea wall watching the horizon. Miguel had been having me watch the shadows on the ocean. Suddenly I began to shake uncontrollably from head to toe. Miguel smiled "that smile" and asked me if I was cold.

I said no and he told me to concentrate on the horizon. I sensed a presence there and began to shake even harder. My mind told me that there was nothing there, but my body knew better. My body was becoming painfully aware of its own mortality. I was terrified, but I could not name my terror. I had never experienced such intense fear. Miguel told me the presence was death and it was just a short distance away. If my body had been able to respond, I am sure I would have run in terror. But I was totally rooted to the spot.

Miguel told me I had nothing to fear except my fear. He told me that my fear fed these inorganic beings and gave them the power to hurt me. He told me I had to learn to control my fear. He told me that ethereal beings feed on emotions just as our physical bodies need food for their nourishment. Miguel said that many inorganic beings will attach themselves energetically to people and feed on their emotions. They have the ability to generate emotions such as fear or anger in human beings. They generate these feelings so they can harvest their food, the emotions. He went on to say that none of these beings could hurt me unless I "fed" them. Once I fed them or believed they could hurt me, I was vulnerable and could actually die. Death often feeds on fear. I didn't want to feed death so I tried, with very little success, to calm down.

He told me death was actually a great teacher. It reminded us to learn and pushed us to strive and grow. Years later when I did the same exercise for my own apprentices, I saw death as a loving and gentle teacher. It comes to welcome us when our time here is done. But at the time I was so overwhelmed by fear that I couldn't experience that loving presence. Death represented nothing but fear. The energy felt like a herd of wild horses pawing the ground, ready to trample me.

As I continued exploring these alternate realities with Miguel, I was forced to look at all my fears and limiting beliefs. I began to feel like I was living a nightmare. Not only did my internal world feel crazy, but my outside world was also falling apart. I now realize that on the physical plane I had begun the process I later learned was called "going through the tunnel."

EXERCISE ONE

This a journey in which you find yourself. If you choose to embark upon this journey, at some point you will have to question all your beliefs. You will have to own and release all of your limitations. It is a journey with freedom as its destination.

At the end of each chapter there will be an exercise and a series of questions. Your answers to these questions are very important. They will assist you in letting go of some of your limiting beliefs so you can begin to see the world in a new way.

You could begin now by asking yourself the following questions. Be as honest with yourself as you can. Try answering these questions more then once. Your answers will change as you do. Give yourself the gift of becoming all you were meant to be. The Great Spirit sees only our perfection, allow yourself to become that perfection.

Be specific, thoroughly discuss any concepts you have about your world. Take some time and really think about your answers to all your questions in this book.

How do you view your world? as perfection when I am not in my fear or emotional reaction

Are you an important part of it or do you feel separate? I am a part

Is it a safe or hostile place? safe

What is your role, are you the hero or the victim? I am both but mostly hero now a survivor

How does your world work, is it random or preordained?

it is preordained but
free will is a part of it

What are you looking for?

personal freedom

Do you want peace of mind, love, or power?

love — with love the rest will
be there

What do you hope to achieve by reading this book?

Greater understanding — another
pt of view

How will you know if you have found it?

I will feel it

How would your life be different?

more personal freedom

What would your life look like?

less drama

Would you be working at the same job? *yes but* *approaching it to more spiritually*

What facts would change about your life?

*no facts only beliefs about
the facts*

What could you do today to improve the quality of your life?

refrain, patience, dreams

THE TUNNEL

*The longest journey we will ever take
is the one in which we find ourselves.*

 I started my symbolic journey into the tunnel one day
when I was meditating with the group. Once again
Miguel placed me in the triangle at the center of the circle.
The triangle represented the trinity of the physical, ethereal,
and spiritual. The outer circle represented the ring of fire. This
ring of fire symbolized the protective band of apprentices
around each Nagual.

As we meditated, I became aware of an opening and felt
drawn towards it. I felt torn between my desire to move forward and my fear of that next step. Most of my being wanted
to run, but I knew I might never muster the courage to proceed if I ran.

I stepped into an opening. Suddenly I found myself inside a
tunnel. Although I was unable to see things clearly, the walls felt

very stifling. My entire being began to react. I felt like I was being drawn down into the tunnel by an irresistible force. I was unable to breathe, the air smelled musty and stale.

Immediately I experienced an intense sense of dread and terror. I wasn't seeing anything, but I sensed danger. I felt like there were horrible things right at the edge of my reality. I could almost see the beings, but when I turned my head to face them they disappeared. Although I couldn't actually see them, the monsters felt like vampires, werewolves, and demons.

I knew I was trapped. At some level I feared I would spend eternity caught in this tunnel. Somehow I knew I would be trapped forever if I tried fighting the experience. Every time I started struggling, the sides seemed to get smaller and it began to smell even mustier, the air smelled dead. I felt claustrophobic, then I sensed something or someone chasing me. I felt like I was losing my mind.

I was running. I felt totally disoriented and lost. Suddenly the tunnel was filled with blind alleys, I had no idea which way to turn. All my fears seemed to be taking on forms. I felt like I was being pursued by hundreds of demons. Their faces were all distorted with anger and fear. Thankfully, off in the distance, I heard Miguel's voice calling us back from the meditation. When I returned to the room I was sweating profusely.

Little did I know that I had started a process that night which would turn my world upside down. I began to feel as if I were in a grade B movie in which all my fears were projected on the screen of my life in living color. It was as if my entire life had an overlay of fear on it. I felt like someone had painted my life gray. The joy was gone, and only fear was left.

I found my fears manifesting in interesting ways. One of my favorite fears was not having enough money. When I did have enough, I was sure I'd lose it (and I usually did). When I was short of money, I was certain I'd never have any more. At the time I was working in sales making excellent money. All of a sudden I seemed unable to sell anything and I lost my job.

Then things happened to me that had never happened in my life before. I seldom got sick; but I got the flu. Then one day I was picking up a bottle of water and I slipped a disc in my back. The pain was unreal. I felt like my body and my life were falling apart.

My dreams were also very intense and bizarre. I frequently found myself in dark alleys being chased. At times I would find myself slipping into other worlds. Our physical laws did not operate in those universes, so the beings there were able to do unbelievable feats. One minute they would seem small and harmless, in the next instant they would become huge and look very fearful. They could walk through walls. Frequently they jumped over me. They also changed form at times. On one occasion, the skin of one of the beings melted off like wax on a candle. I can still see the eye oozing down its face.

Sometimes Miguel or his mother would come and take me on journeys during my dreams. They would teach me the most amazing things. When I would awaken, I would remember my sense of awe at the information, but I could not remember the information itself. As the years have passed, though, I have remembered much of it, like how to work with people in dreams, heal people in the dream-state, and shift forms. I still have an active dream life.

During this time, all my old fears and paranoia came to the surface. Some mornings I would wake up uncertain of whether I had been dreaming or if the dreams were real. The boundaries between reality and dreams seemed to be dissolving. I was terrified. I felt like I was in limbo. I tried to hold on to all my external safety nets—people, places, and things—but whatever I clung to seemed to dissolve before my very eyes.

My mind had a terrible time with this whole process. There were no neat little boxes to put my life into anymore. My mind's old explanations no longer worked. I felt like I was in uncharted territory. Although at times it was a real high to experience this new reality, at other times it was totally unsettling. Sometimes I wasn't sure if I wanted to continue, or even if I could. But a part of me kept pushing me forward.

Frequently during my studies my mind would try to convince me that I had found "the answer." As soon as I believed that I was trapped in the tunnel again. The tunnel was formed by my beliefs. Whenever I felt I had the answer I stopped looking towards my spiritual center and slid back into the tunnel. It took me years to realize that as long as I stayed in a position of humility and not knowing the answer, I remained teachable and free.

Later one of the other students explained the tunnel to me. The tunnel is really a symbol for the process of facing all our limiting beliefs and fears. Reality, as we perceive it, is an illusion. Going through the tunnel is a process of removing our illusions and experiencing our existence on a pure energy level. It takes time.

As I proceeded through the tunnel, I saw how most of my life was an illusion or delusion of my mind. I realized that what happened out there didn't really matter. What mattered was what I told myself about what happened. I began to realize that there actually was no "out there." Out there was merely a reflection of what was going on internally. If I was angry and not willing to experience my anger, I ran into a lot of situations that "caused me to feel angry." For example, I had a new commissioned sales job. Every week my pay check was short, so I would march upstairs and rage at my bosses. That was an expensive way to access my anger.

I began to see how the universe was a complex series of causes and effects. Later in my studies, I saw those causes and effects as a web of energy that binds us to the past in an unhealthy manner until we are willing to let go.

The tunnel was really a process of reviewing the past, seeing what beliefs I had that were no longer serving me, and then making the necessary changes. With my sales job, once I released my belief that my money came from my bosses rather than from the universe, I got a much better paying position. If I had realized this concept at the beginning of the process, I am sure my life would have been easier. But I kept focusing on the fears rather than the beliefs that caused the fears.

The entire process was very painful and mentally stressful. I was unable and unwilling to ask for help. No matter how much pain I was in I remained stoic. My mind wanted to do it its way. I manifested my beliefs about not being lovable and my need to be right in a very painful manner. I allowed myself to be victimized by the whole process. It took me years to release these fears. I didn't realize until then that 90 percent of the struggle was between my ears.

During my journey through the tunnel, I also often felt powerless, helpless, and hopeless. I didn't believe I was the creator in my life. The truth was that I wasn't willing to let go of my role of victim. As a child I had learned to get attention by playing "poor me."

As an adult I was doing the same thing. By not looking at my beliefs, I could feel like a victim to my feelings and the situations they created. For example, when I didn't have any money, rather than getting an extra job or making more sales, I whined about having no money.

In my studies with Miguel this behavior was a real hindrance and liability. It caused me a great deal of emotional pain. For instance, as I began to travel to alternate realities in my meditations, I would often come back with inorganic beings attached to my psyche. They would cause intense emotional pain. These beings fed on the emotions of anger or fear. To get rid of them, all I had to do was ask them to leave. But I was so invested in my role of victim, I had to run to Miguel to remove them. In the meantime, they were able to terrify me.

At one point, I remember going to class fully convinced that I had to kill myself. I was filled with rage and would not allow anyone to talk to me or even come close. Miguel sat on the other side of the room and smiled at me. In that instant I felt pure rage. My only desire was to kill him. I had never felt such hate before. I had no idea what was going on. It took every ounce of my strength to remain in that room. When Miguel said it was time to meditate, I wanted to run out of there as fast as I could. I was so immersed in the feelings that I was totally unaware that something was amiss.

The lights dimmed and we began our meditation. Miguel sat directly in front of me. I was puzzled, I had never seen him do that before. I was growing angrier by the moment and the last thing I wanted to do was get quiet and meditate. Miguel began to stare intently into my eyes. I thought I saw hate coming out of his eyes and my anger turned into terror. I closed my eyes and I immediately began spinning. I heard garbled voices off in the distance, they sounded very angry and loud.

Suddenly Miguel and I were standing in a field next to a beautiful lake. We mounted a horse and he began swimming with us on his back. I felt at peace and very comfortable, like I had been here before. Just as suddenly I found myself sitting back in the temple once again staring into Miguel's eyes. He asked me if I was alright. I felt fine and told him so.

During the break he came over and smiled. He said that I had come in with a very angry being securely attached to me. He laughed as he talked about watching it stare at him all during class. He told me I was advancing nicely and that this being had been very large and powerful. I looked puzzled and he laughed again. He told me it took a powerful wizard to catch such a large creature. I told him that I hadn't caught him, he had caught me. Then I realized that I could change my perspective and take my power back from those pesky things. He nodded with approval. I felt a little less afraid.

The most uncomfortable part of going through the tunnel for me was actually experiencing my feelings. As a child I grew up in an alcoholic household where it was extremely unsafe to have feelings at all. As a result, I frequently tried to think my way through feeling rather than just feeling the emotions. I kept trying to explain away my emotions with comments like, "If I were truly spiritual, I would be happy, not angry, or fearful."

Eventually I felt like I had no other options. I had run out of places to hide. My mind had no more excuses. The situations in my life had become intense enough that I became willing to experience my feelings. I caught on. Rather than having someone break into my apartment to access my fear, I could look at my fear first. I began to seek out my emotions. When I began to feel uncomfortable I would search out why. My journey through the tunnel became a lot easier. A huge shift took place in that tunnel. I began to move towards happiness rather than moving away from pain. Slowly I began to take back my power. I stopped being a victim.

I also began to realize that my sense of safety had to come from within; the outside things kept letting me down and going away. So I began to look within myself, and I stopped trying to fix the outside. I reassessed my beliefs. I realized that I had an underlying belief that the world was out to get me. Once I changed that belief my experiences became much easier. My "lessons" became more gentle, and my life got lighter.

One of the other apprentices explained to me that the tunnel was the first battle in our bid for our personal power. It is a battle between our mind, with all its limitations, and our inner essence, or spiritual center. By nature we are totally free beings, so any restrictions or limitations are stifling. That is why we push ourselves and go through the tunnel. We want to free ourselves of our limitations.

In a sense our whole life is a process of going through our personal tunnels. Eventually, however, instead of being trapped in a tunnel with only an entrance and an exit, we regain our ability to choose to go left or right, as well as forward or backwards.

EXERCISE TWO

You could begin your journey into the tunnel by exploring your emotions. What "makes you" angry, happy, sad, or frightened? Begin to look for the internal causes rather then blaming external events. What limiting beliefs are you still holding on to? An excellent way to begin your exploration is to keep a journal. Write about your emotions.

List all the different emotions you have felt over the past week. Then ask yourself the following questions about an event that "caused" you to feel those emotions.

What was happening, what event or events were talking place?

What were you telling yourself about the event or events?

Were you saying things like: "Things will never change." "I'll always be like this." "I am going to lose." "I am not going to get what I want." "I may get hurt?"

Spend some time asking yourself about your internal dialog. What do you tell yourself on a daily basis about your world?

Do the same thing with each of the emotions you have felt over the past week. We are rarely upset for the reasons we think we are. We are actually upset by the things we tell ourselves about what has happened.

Over the next few weeks b—
life. Observe your mind and
everything that is happenin—
mind usually lies to you.

Our thoughts are so hab—
them. People seldom question th—
their mind is saying as fact. It is not fac—
you change your opinions, your life will cha—

What is your favorite emotion?

Which one do you feel most often?

The one you feel most often is really your favorite emotion or you wouldn't feel it all the time. What did your mind tell you about that?

◆◆◆◆◆◆◆◆◆◆◆◆◆ 𝟛 ◆◆◆◆◆◆◆◆◆◆◆◆◆

THE NATURE OF REALITY

We are an energy as vast as the sky.
Unfortunately we often believe that we are the clouds.

As my studies continued with Miguel, the structure of the classes shifted. At first they had been a combination of one-on-one lessons and classes with the other apprentices. For some reason, Miguel fostered a great deal of competition among the apprentices which made it difficult for me to express my fears and ask questions.

After the holidays the classes were opened up to the public. These new classes allowed me to have verbal explanations for many of my experiences. I began to have words for experiences like the tunnel and concepts like the human egg.

Miguel first articulated his ideas about the nature of reality and the concept of the human egg one night in February. The temple was filled with a variety of people. No one knew what would be taught. But, as always, we were all curious and nervous.

Miguel was generally late, so people sat and fidgeted around. Miguel finally arrived and sat on the floor. Some of the other apprentices seemed jealous about sharing him with other people. He smiled graciously and the class began.

Miguel had begun to master English. Haltingly in broken English he explained the nature of reality and the human form. He started out with the following story:

Suppose one day you woke up in a room where there were windows and lots of buttons and switches, but no exit. Out of curiosity you would probably start playing with the switches and buttons. Eventually you would begin to notice that a certain lever would move an object. Later you found out that the object was called a finger. You also began to notice that if you expelled air, you could make a loud noise and a large being would come and take care of you. As time went on, you became totally fascinated with how the system operated. Eventually you forgot you were an energy inside that room, and you began to believe you were the room.

He went on to explain that part of our lesson in this world was to remember what we really were. The purpose of life was to "break this reality" and go beyond the illusion of duality. We are here to remember that the essence of who we are is an energy that is completely free and expansive. We are uncomfortable when we are cut off from that freedom. The limitations of the physical universe push us to grow and evolve.

He pointed to various objects in the room and went on to say that they were all composed of atoms. Those atoms can be further broken down until, ultimately, all that is left is pure energy. At that level there is just energy. There is no separation.

That energy has consciousness. That consciousness is pure love. It is totally expansive, universal, and eternal. It is infinite. You can never go beyond its limits because of its nature. We are all part of it and of each other.

He then discussed the human brain. He likened it to a computer. The brain is an amazingly complex machine. It is able to organize information and store the memories of everything we have ever experienced. Our brains are memory storage units that operate in conjunction with our physical senses.

When our eyes perceive an object, they really "see" a mass of whirling energy. The brain encodes that energy pattern as an object. We actually have to learn how to see. All solid objects are actually more space than solid matter. Our brain just tells us they are solid. The page you are now reading is really mostly vacant space.

When our eyes transmit energy to our brain, it records that energy along with the emotions we are feeling at the time. Each piece of information in our brain has both an emotional component and action component. Our memories of even inanimate objects have an emotion attached to them. For example, if the first time we saw a dog it bit us, then each time we saw a dog we would experience a twinge of fear.

Eventually when we see something our brain searches our memory banks. If we have seen or experienced a person, place, or thing in the past, we recall our memory of that experience. Even if there is only a vague similarity, we still replay the memory rather than experience reality as it is.

He went on to explain how reality is an illusion of our mind. Reality is totally colored by our beliefs and experiences. Even-

tually we seldom experience reality at all. We just react to memories from our past that are superimposed over today's events.
We are no longer free to choose. We are controlled by our emotions, past behaviors, and beliefs.

Life, in a sense, is a process of stepping further and further
away from the truth of who and what we are. At some point in
our life if we are lucky we begin to wake up and begin remembering who we are. That is what this training is about—regain-
ing our personal freedom. Our freedom is easier to regain when
we understand the nature of ourselves and the universe. And,
when we look at ourselves and the world as an energy system,
freedom is easier to attain.

The universe is a reflection of ourselves. When we understand our nature, we begin to understand the nature of the universe. During our limited life spans, it would be impossible to
explore and completely understand the nature of the universe.
Understanding the nature of ourselves is an attainable goal.

Our body is actually composed of several different energy
types or levels (see Figure 3-1). These energies are of different
wave lengths. One way to understand the need for these varying energies is to think of a light bulb. If you had a six-volt light
bulb and plugged it into a 220-volt circuit, it would blow out
immediately. But, if you used a series of transformers to step
down or lower the electricity, you could successfully use the
bulb in the 220-volt system. In a sense, the energies in our bodies also need to be stepped down. Spiritual energy in its pure
form cannot exist on the physical plane. For our spirits to exist
on this physical plane, we need the ethereal body to lower the
intensity of that energy.

Physical energy only perceives physical energy, ethereal energy perceives ethereal energy, and spiritual energy interacts with spiritual energy. We manifest our reality from the spiritual level, but that energy is filtered through all the emotional baggage that is stored in our physical and ethereal bodies. Those filters allow our reality to reflect accurately our core beliefs. As we change our beliefs, we change our life experiences.

Figure 3-1 represents the human form. On an energy level, a human being looks like an incredibly beautiful luminescent egg. The aura is the beginning of this energy field. Fibers of energy flow around and through this egg. Some of them represent blockages such as disease. Others represent beliefs.

The slashes on the diagram represent the various pieces of information that are stored in our brain. When viewed closely, each bit of information is composed of an emotional and action, or informational, component. In a normal human being, two components are connected and act in unison.

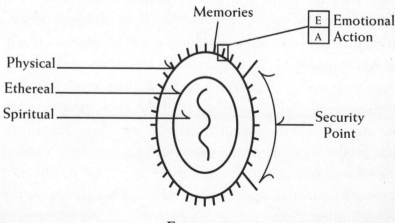

FIGURE 3-1

In a person who has broken this reality, such as a Nagual or great teachers like Buddha, Lao Tzu, or Jesus, those two components have been separated. Energetically their eggs (see Figure 3-2) would look like this:

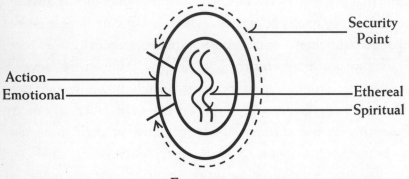

FIGURE 3-2

As you can see in the diagram, the action and emotional components are totally separated. Their ethereal body has also changed. They know they are not their physical body so their ethereal body now resembles their spiritual body.

As I sat there listening, it was wonderful to finally have words for some of the experiences I had been having. In a meditation one day I had seen an old girl friend of mine as an egg. She was shaped like a large egg, but she was totally luminescent. There were fibers of light running throughout her body. They shimmered and danced. In some places the fibers came together and formed intersections similar to hubs on a wheel. I later realized that the intersections were her power points. I was amazed at how beautiful she was at an energy level.

At the time I had a great deal of anger towards her because she had stolen a large sum of money from me. Next to her, in the same form, stood some of my fellow apprentices. At that energy level they all looked the same, even though I had no anger towards the apprentices. The only visible difference was in the arrangement of the fibers.

I was then shown my egg, and I could see my anger as a jagged, disjointed energy within my structure. I saw how the anger I had towards her affected me but not her. Seeing the stress the anger caused to my system made me review some of my beliefs about the usefulness of anger in my life. Now listening to Miguel explain the human egg made me reflect on this experience in a new light.

I began to understand more clearly what Miguel did when he "worked on my power points." During the class meditations, Miguel and some of the more advanced apprentices would go around and work in people's power points. When they channeled energy into you, it felt like your body was vibrating. At times I would feel like my world had begun to spin. Frequently I would feel nauseous. Often, after Miguel would work on me, I would experience fear or anger about something. At times the emotions would feel overwhelming.

I now realized that within a person's energy field there are points that, when manipulated, can rearrange some of the fibers. These fibers are tied to our beliefs. When they are manipulated our beliefs are shaken up. Any behaviors attached to those beliefs begin to rise to the surface of our reality.

By working on my power points Miguel separated the action from the emotion. I was left with emotion and no action to blame it on. This allowed me the freedom to explore the feeling more in depth. When I was feeling enough emotional pain, I would begin to look at the beliefs behind those feelings.

That night after Miguel's lecture, we did our usual group meditation. I was asked to sit in the triangle again. I felt the energy begin to swirl around the circle. It became stronger and stronger, until I found myself carried up out of the room.

I found myself walking through a field. I knew I was in a separate reality because of the sky. The skies in those realities always looked flat to me, like poorly constructed movie sets, and could be gray or pink in color.

At first the field was empty and flat. I was feeling a bit disoriented and lost. The entire world was eerily silent, I couldn't even hear myself breathing. Then I began to see bodies. At first there were only a few, but after a time they were everywhere. They were mangled and badly wounded. I felt like I was the only thing moving in the universe. I wanted to run but couldn't. I was very relieved when I heard Miguel's voice calling me back.

After the meditation the group would share their experiences. Most of the other people in the group reported seeing stars and shapes. I felt like I must have done something wrong. My meditation was far from cheerful. Later Miguel told me I had merely seen the suffering of the spirits that got lost on their way home. I left class that night feeling very unsettled.

EXERCISE THREE

Becoming aware of power points and being able to see people as energy forms is a matter of practice. You could begin by meditating and concentrating on seeing a person's essence. Allow yourself to relax and gently begin thinking about someone you know, preferably a person you are emotionally neutral about.

Allow them to quietly drift into your consciousness. Breathe deeply and mentally begin to sense them. How do they feel? What kinds of thoughts enter your consciousness?

Remain open and aware of how you are feeling and what you are thinking. Once you get a clear image of the person, you can step into their body and see how it feels. Ask yourself questions about them as you stand inside their body.

Once you become proficient at using this technique, you can use it to get information about various subjects. If you are taking an exam, visualize your teacher and ask them the answer to the question. You'll be amazed at the information you can get.

Fortunately it is hard to get emotionally charged information. It is almost impossible to invade a person's privacy in this way, especially if there are any emotions attached to the information you are trying to gather.

Besides just sensing people, you can also learn how to see a person's aura or the beginning of the human egg. Doing this is easy but takes a great deal of practice. Our minds tend to censor our ability to see those energy wavelengths. You can start by sitting in a dim room with someone sitting opposite you against a white surface. Concentrate on the area around their head and shoulders. Don't look directly at them, look beyond them at an area a few feet behind them. Unfocus your eyes and look at the person softly. Breathe slowly and deeply. Let yourself relax and let go of your mind. Let yourself feel like you're about to fall asleep. After a time, you will begin to see the person's aura.

What are your beliefs about who and what you are?

How would you describe yourself? Are you your body?

How would you define your spiritual essence?

If you thought of yourself as pure energy, what would you be like?

4

THE UNIVERSE

*There is and there is illusion
and that is all there is.*

 The following week my fears continued unabated. I
found fears from my childhood as well as unknown
fears rising to the surface of my consciousness. I spent the week
walking around with a general feeling of dread and discomfort.
These feelings reminded me of how I felt when I walked home
at dusk in the late fall as a child. The trees would cast odd shadows and make strange creaky noises as their bare branches
rubbed together. I can remember walking along looking at the
warm glow coming from the houses that I passed. I would experience intense feelings of loneliness and misgiving.

As I approached the temple that night, it was a cold and
rainy California night. The only thing missing from the scene
was the smell of dead leaves under my feet and the sound of
creaking branches. I felt the same sense of dread I had felt as a

child. I was not looking forward to the damp chill that awaited me inside the temple. I looked up at the sky that night and began to muse about my childhood fascination with the sky.

I was always curious about the stars. Even though we lived in New York City, I always felt an incredible sense of wonder and awe when I looked up at the stars. I was certain they were really made of magic. The first time we went to visit my grandparents in Pennsylvania, I was shocked by the number of stars. I drove my parents crazy with endless questions about how the world worked and why there were so many more stars here than at home. I would stand there totally transfixed, oblivious to everyone around me. My mother would call and call, but I never heard her, I was lost in another world.

When I was seven, I remember being confronted with the concept of infinity. I had never been so terrified in my entire life. The idea of the blackness of space going on forever was the most frightening thing I could ever have imagined. I spent many nights lying awake because of that fear. Eventually, as children do, I "forgot" about the fear and got on with the business of growing up. It wasn't until years later, when I ran across a specific geometry that explained infinity in an enclosed system, that I was able to partially put that fear to rest.

As Miguel described the universe that night, I felt the same fear I had felt as a child. In that moment I was again a terrified seven-year-old looking at the night sky in absolute terror because I had just found out that it went on forever. Eventually that fear began to abate. I realized that I had finally come full circle. As I stood and looked at that starry night sky and again saw only the magic, I realized I was no longer afraid of infinity.

Slowly, Miguel began to explain his concepts about the nature of our infinite universe. He drew the following diagram (Figure 4-1) and explained that the universe is also composed of three forms of energy, the physical, ethereal, and spiritual.

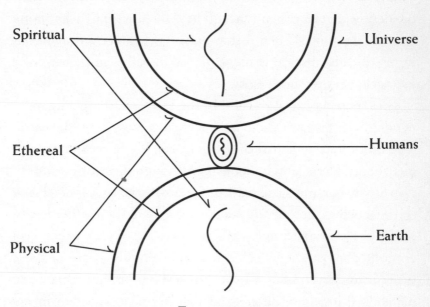

FIGURE 4-1

Whenever we examine any object, we always find that it is composed of atoms. Physicists have found that, as they continue to split atoms, they ultimately find that they are composed of pure energy. They have found that, as the objects get smaller, they are also affected by the expectations of the observer. If the observer expects it to act like a particle, it will, if the observer expects it to act like a wave, it will also do that. This implies that this energy has consciousness. Miguel went on to say that its consciousness was one of pure love. At that energy level, we are all one, there is no separation or duality.

The beauty of this system is that it allows us to have the ability to view various levels simultaneously. In human beings there are a variety of cells. There are liver cells, brain cells, skin cells, etc. Each type of cell functions in a specific manner independently of the other types. They all function in harmony most of the time. When disharmony exists among the various forms of cells, disease is present. A skin cell is not aware of a liver cell, yet they both exist.

In a sense we are also "cells" of the earth, we all operate independently but we are also part of a greater ecosystem, the earth. The earth, in turn, is part of the universe. We also exist on various energy levels simultaneously. Although most of our attention is on our physical reality, we also exist as ethereal and spiritual beings. Frequently we are unaware of these other levels, just as the liver and finger cells are unaware of each other. As I continued my studies, I often became painfully aware of these other levels. Eventually I began to realize that my fears often manifested on the ethereal and that my peace resided in my connection to my spiritual level.

Figure 4-2 is an ancient symbol of the entire universe. It is the sun with seven arms or rays. In its entirety, it represents the whole universe. It also allows us to begin to see or sense the interdependence and harmony that exists in the universe. Humans are in the middle because they contain all the various forms of energy.

As I sat there listening to Miguel describe these concepts, I only understood them on an intellectual level. Later I came to understand these concepts as reality and as a way of life. That

energy is so much more than words can possibly convey. As I
began to experience this energy, I realized that I was unable
to actually describe it. As soon as I began to use words to
define it, it changed. It seems to be a mass of contradictions.
It is infinite, eternal, and immortal. It is amazingly gentle, yet
powerful. It is immense, yet it exists within even the smallest
object. It is totally non-invasive. It will never say no to us, and
it is always there. As soon as you name it, it is gone and yet
still there.

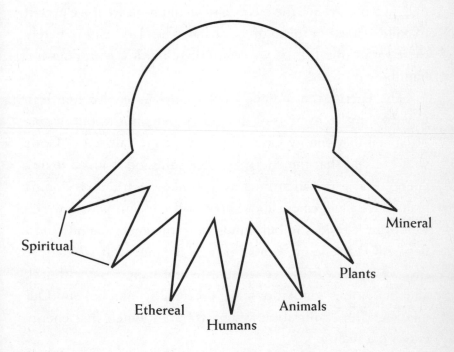

FIGURE 4-2

Miguel just referred to it as the energy. He said that the "old ones" had wasted a great deal of energy trying to understand it. Miguel went on to explain that this energy was something we had to experience for ourselves. There were no words to explain this energy, it just exists. The closest my mind ever came to understanding it was when I compared it to electricity. Electricity exists within our homes, yet we are often totally unaware of it. Whenever we want to use electricity, we merely have to tap into it by turning on a switch or plugging in an appliance. We cannot use electricity directly or it would kill us, yet it definitely adds to the quality of our lives. If we were to plug in a power saw, the electricity would not care if we used it to build a house or to cut off our hand. The electricity is merely there for us to utilize as we see fit. It is limitless so it does not limit how it is used.

The energy that composes the universe is also limitless. Once we try to name it or describe it, we limit it, but people often call that energy God. Miguel began to talk about God's will. He said that the energy people call God is just a loving energy that exists all around us. It is like electricity, it doesn't really have a judgement about how we use it. The way in which we utilize it resides in our mind not in the energy's consciousness. All that energy wants for us is happiness. If we believe that we are unworthy, we will create our "happiness" with lack and limitation. Limitations are created by our beliefs. Our minds act like a filtration system through which that energy enters our reality.

Miguel went on to explain that everything in our universe is composed of this energy. Our belief that we are separate from this energy creates our belief in duality which, in turn, gives our reality physical form. Our minds perceive this energy, but they believe they are separate so they see the separation. Our minds see a swirling mass of electrons and translates that mass into an object, such as a chair. A chair is really just that energy, it is not solid at all. Yet our minds believe it is solid, so we see it as solid. What we see and experience is always a direct reflection of what we believe. This page is actually mostly vacant space, yet we perceive it as solid. We spend lifetimes finding out who and what we are not, until we finally remember that we really are one with that energy.

My mind found it impossible to understand this explanation. It flew in the face of so many concepts I had come to understand. Eventually I found this method of describing the universe very effective. It allowed me to begin to see beyond the illusion of duality. It also gave me the freedom to explore how our world operates without imposing a lot of limitations and rules. At first I found the lack of rules unsettling, but as I proceeded on my path it became so much easier. I no longer found it necessary to argue for my limiting beliefs quite so vigorously. My life began to have a greater sense of harmony.

I was beginning to understand what Miguel meant when he said that there was no out there. That out there was merely a reflection of what is going on internally. Miguel often stressed that in studying the microcosm, our body was a more efficient way of studying the macrocosm, our universe. The universe is so immense that it would take life times to fully understand it, but we can understand ourselves if we exert enough discipline. Eventually I began to understand how I created my reality. In the process I began to have a clearer concept about the functioning of the universe.

Our minds are an incredibly powerful filtration system. Miguel related the story about the first encounter the Incas had with the Spaniards. The Holy Men of the tribes had dreamed about the white men coming in their large boats to conquer their people. When the Spaniards arrived, the majority of people were unable to see the large boats. They could only see the small boats the Spaniards used to come ashore. The priest had dreamed about the large boats, so they were able to see them. Eventually they got the people to see the large boats by telling them what to look for and where to look.

Our minds limit our experience of life by limiting our perceptions. The filtering system used by our minds is our beliefs. Whatever we believe, we are able to experience. That ability to filter reality is why our minds are our enemies when we are exploring our spiritually or the ethereal realms. It is new territory, so our minds refuse to admit those realms exist. As I proceeded on my path, I found that my mind also tended to go to any lengths to avoid change.

EXERCISE FOUR

You can easily begin to feel this energy or the life force. Sit quietly for a few minutes and concentrate on your breathing. Breathe deeply and rhythmically. Quiet your mind and relax.

Hold your hands about six inches apart and concentrate on the area between them. Really "feel" that area, place your consciousness there. Very slowly begin moving your hands in and out. Continue to breathe slowly and play with the movement of your hands. Notice any variation in the way the area feels. Vary the speed and the distance you move your hands. Let yourself "feel" with your heart or your inner self.

After a few moments you will begin to "feel" something there. Some people describe the feeling as sticky, others feel a resistance, while others say they see a ball of energy. Each person senses it differently, let yourself explore how you sense it. Quiet your mind's opinions as much as possible. However you perceive it, that is the life force. Be gentle with yourself. It may take a little patience, but you will feel it.

Our definitions of events, people, and ideas affect our experience of them. For example, if we decide we don't trust someone, no matter what they did, we would doubt their motives. Someone else could do the same things and we would not mistrust them if we had decided they were honest.

What is your concept of God?

Is the energy unconditionally loving or does it somehow judge you?

Think about your universe, is it friendly and supportive or do you perceive it as dangerous?

Do you feel you have to protect yourself and your belongings?

Is life a struggle or is it an adventure?

Define the following words:

love

power

spirituality

abundance

limitations

karma

beliefs

truth

money

ego

magic

miracles

success

failure

Are your definitions limiting your experience of life or expanding it? Change your definitions until they can support a life
filled with ease.

5

THE SECURITY POINT AND CHANGE

To say "I believe" is to limit our experience.
Our limitations are ours if we believe in them.

As my studies progressed one fact became painfully obvious, my mind would much rather be right than happy. Time and time again I found myself making choices that caused me pain. I was amazed at the complexities of my mind and the way it insisted on doing things the old way. One day I asked Miguel about this phenomenon, he smiled and began to talk to me about our security point (see Figure 5-1 on page 52).

Our security point is the limited area of our reality that is familiar. We feel safe there because we know what to expect. If we stay within that narrow band of life experiences, we remain comfortable, unchallenged, and also frequently unhappy. Our minds will go to any length to maintain this status quo. I have seen clients work very hard and get right to the brink of success, only to have their minds make them return to old beliefs.

51

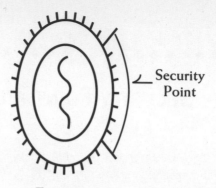

Security
Point

FIGURE 5-1

Our security point works in the same manner as the comfort zone in a heating system. In heating or cooling systems there is a variance in temperature that is referred to as a comfort zone. A thermostat will allow the temperature to rise and fall a predetermined amount of degrees before the system reacts. If the variance for the system is two degrees and we set the thermostat at 68, the temperature may go up to 70 and fall to 66 before the heater turns on or off. It is called a comfort zone because it is assumed that the occupants of the space will be unaware of the changes in temperature.

Our security point works in the same manner and each person's security point is defined differently. In order to feel secure, some people must have a job, for some it is a lover, and for others it is a certain amount of money in the bank. What our minds define as secure varies from person to person as well as from day to day. The only thing constant about our mind's definition of security is that the elements of that security are always things that lie outside of ourselves. Our mind's security is always related to people, places, or things beyond our control.

As long as our sense of security lies outside ourselves we are doomed to search for security and happiness, yet never find it. It will always lie just beyond our reach. The rules constantly change. As soon as we achieve our mind's definition of safety, the definition changes. Our minds are worthy opponents once we step onto our spiritual path. Our minds fear their mortality, so they act like cheap magicians. They will always tell us to look over there for our happiness, when our happiness actually resides in our connection to our spiritual center.

Our minds work like a computer, garbage in—garbage out. The mind will go to any length to protect our security point, to maintain the status quo. Unfortunately that also limits our experience of life. Within our security point resides all the experiences we are comfortable with. If we have never been on an airplane and we have negative beliefs about adventure, we would not be able to go on a plane unless we expanded our security point. The entire circumference of the human egg represents all of the life experiences that are available to us. As we can see by the diagram (see Figure 5-1), the area within our security point is only a fraction of that whole.

As long as we are willing to assist our mind in defending our security point, we are severely limited. Conflict arises because our mind assisted us in surviving by setting up these limitations in the first place. As we attempt to change, we are challenging our basic survival skills. We are going up against the very beliefs we came into this world to resolve.

In a sense our beliefs are the walls of our security point. Our minds use our beliefs as their guide lines. Whatever we believe, we will manifest. As my studies continued, I realized that 100 percent of my life experiences reside in my mind. No situation in my life is inherently good or bad, pleasant or stressful. My mind defines what I experience. My beliefs dictate what I think and feel about any situation.

At one point during my studies I was asked to move out of the condo I was living in because it had been sold. I felt like a victim and was very unhappy about the change. I had a dog, actually a puppy, and finding a place for both of us to live was not easy. I scanned the papers daily and cruised the neighborhoods. I was convinced the situation was hopeless and a disaster.

After looking for an apartment for several weeks, I found a cute one bedroom a half a block from the beach. It was only slightly more expensive than the one I was living in, and it was wonderful. There was a heated pool and the landlord even loved my dog. The situation my mind had judged so harshly turned out to be a real blessing.

Our security point is like a steel door that slams shut every time we try to go beyond our limitations. There are several ways to circumvent our security point. The easiest way to achieve permanent change is to work on a different energy level. After all it is impossible to fix a broken computer with a broken computer. It is difficult to correct our beliefs and to change our behaviors if we are working purely on the physical level. Once we tap into another energy level, change becomes much easier.

When we meditate, several things begin to happen. As we quiet the mind and relax, we begin to go into an altered state of consciousness (see Figure 5-2). As we shift gears mentally, we open a door to the ethereal. We actually allow energy to flow in from the universe. That is why frequently while medi-

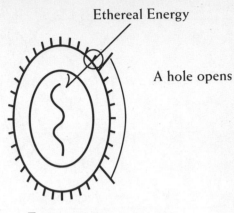

FIGURE 5-2

tating we have profound insights. We have tapped into the collective unconsciousness. We can use this energy to institute changes in our psyche, we can use it to change our mind's limited view of the world.

At certain times in our lives, we seem to make profound shifts in our beliefs without any conscious decision on our parts. Spontaneously we suddenly experience life differently. Our behaviors change dramatically, seemingly for no reason at all. What has happened is that our spiritual self has intervened (see Figure 5-3). This usually only happens if our very survival is threatened. We always have free will, but at times our spiritual self will save us from ourselves. It will not force us to change, but it will allow the change to take place without our conscious effort. This type of change will also occur if we consciously decide to align ourselves with our spiritual center.

After a great deal of struggle, I learned to constantly ask my spiritual essence for guidance and direction. From that viewpoint, I realized that I have a much clearer view about what was

FIGURE 5-3

really going on in my life. Our spiritual essence only wants us to be happy and feel loved. It will always respect our free will and allow us to be miserable.

Another way we can change is when we have a major life crisis or displacement. Frequently when someone looses their home, job, or a close relationship, their outlook on life will shift dramatically. A close brush with death will also instigate these changes. In a case like this, our lives seem to be changed through an act of providence. This type of change often feels totally out of our control from the perspective of our mind. This type of change became my least favorite (see Figure 5-4).

Frequently as a child I experienced these types of shifts. When I was in high school, our home burned to the ground and we lost everything. For a long time afterward I was unable to allow myself to become attached to anything. At times in my life I thought my sense of detachment was very negative, but as I studied with Miguel I began to realize it could also be a blessing.

As my security point began to expand I began to realize that my happiness resides within myself. I now know that my happi-

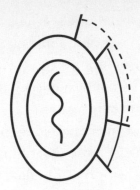

Our security point shifts due to a trauma in our life.

FIGURE 5-4

ness is totally dependent upon my attitude. I can be as happy as I decide to be. All I have to do is change what I am telling myself. My mind will generally choose to view things negatively. It is my choice whether or not to listen.

As we continued to talk, Miguel began to push on my power points. As he did this, he channeled ethereal energy into my body. Slowly his voice began to fade into the background, and I realized that I was no longer there in the room with him. Whenever that happened I always felt like I was drifting backwards and floating up a tunnel. Drifting in that tunnel was effortless. I was definitely not in control, I was along for the ride. First I would feel very tired, then I would begin to drift mentally and feel like I was dozing off. The next thing I knew I would be in another reality.

This time I found myself in a place that was pure energy. It was very peaceful, yet I knew it was time for me to move on. I realized that I had moved back in time to a period just prior to my birth. I was deciding whether or not to reincarnate. The place I found myself in that instant is hard to describe. It wasn't really a place as much as it was a feeling. I was beyond time and space as we know it. I was pure consciousness, I was everywhere and nowhere. Time had little meaning. I knew if I chose to step back into my body I would experience time, but because time did not exist, it didn't really matter.

As I previewed my life I saw a lot of pain and struggle, but I also saw growth. I had a sense that, if I decided to reincarnate when I was finished with that life time, I would be closer to knowing myself. These thoughts made no sense. Why would I ever want to leave this peaceful place? I knew, yet I doubted that I could be freer. I was puzzled. Suddenly I found myself back in the temple with Miguel. He had that smile on his face. He asked me what I had seen. I told him.

Miguel began to talk about reincarnation. He frequently stressed our freedom to choose everything, including our parents. In the past I used that ability to choose as an excuse to abuse myself emotionally. My mind still had responsibility mixed up with being at fault. Miguel would just smile and shake his head when I would get into that line of thinking. On this day I began to see the difference. I could see how those choices I had made were actually choices to be freer and to be one step closer to experiencing a sense of oneness with my spiritual center. I was moving towards the light, not punishing myself for being bad.

Miguel drew a diagram similar to Figure 5-5. He said that when we die, we slowly lose our physical form. At first we continue to believe that we are our physical body, so our ethereal body retains its human form. Eventually we realize that we are an energy and we lose our ethereal body as well. At that point we are ready to reincarnate. The various slashes on our

Death   Reincarnation

FIGURE 5-5

bodies represent our beliefs. These can be an attitude such as believing we don't deserve love. As a matter of fact, we are unaware that love is available to us, so we are attracted to parents that have a difficult time showing love. Then, as our life progresses, we continue to prove our belief that we are unlovable. Our challenge in any life time is to go beyond our limiting beliefs. It is our job to learn how to love ourselves unconditionally. The very things we came here to learn in this lifetime always reside beyond our security point.

Miguel was constantly challenging his students to go beyond their security point. He challenged me that day by informing me I would be teaching a class that night on the security point. I was terrified. That night, as the students filed into the temple, I sat there next to Miguel with my heart pounding in my throat. The class was rather uneventful, but the meditation afterwards was very powerful for me.

In the meditation I once again found myself in that peaceful place where I existed only as pure energy. I was everywhere and nowhere again. The best way I can describe it is that I felt like I was standing on top of a mountain, but there was no mountain. I was on a cliff, but the cliff wasn't there. Below me there were millions of stars. They were all connected by webs of energy. I began to see the entire universe as an energy web. Everyone and everything was connected by filaments of light.

Occasionally there were areas of greater concentration, it looked like little balls of light with spider webs in between them. I saw how every move being made affected the whole. Even though each movement affected the whole, there was no concern because no matter how any thing moved the whole remained balanced. There was a great sense of balance and harmony. If a light went out in one place, it came back on someplace else. There was only love and peace, no drama. It was a beautiful light show filled with love. There was no right and wrong, no judgement of any kind. It was just an extremely complex spider web blowing in a gentle breeze. It looked like a beautiful tapestry of light, always moving yet always finished, whole and complete. Time did not seem to exist, everything was happening all at once. It was magnificent.

Slowly I began to realize that I was seeing the world as it truly is. My "normal" perspective was incorrect. I could choose to experience my life from this perspective and life would be a lot easier. "But how?" I wondered. I heard the thought, "By relaxing and remembering we are one. Only the love is real, everything else is an illusion." When I opened my eyes Miguel was smiling gently and he slowly nodded his head. I felt a sense of peace I had never known before. The knot I always had in my stomach, the one I never knew I had, was gone.

EXERCISE FIVE

We are creatures of habit. We do the same things in the same way, time after time. Our habits and routines allow us to feel safe, but they also help maintain our limited perspective. As long as we retain the status quo, our security point remains intact.

Try doing things differently just to see what happens. Go to work a new way, sleep on the other side of the bed, put your clothes on in a different order, eat at different times. Just shake up your routines and see what happens. Your perspective of the world might change and your security point will shift.

If we keep doing the same thing in the same way, we will continue to get the same results. This is especially true of our thinking. Of all of our behaviors, our habitual thought patterns cause the most pain in our lives. If you think in a certain way or you hold onto certain beliefs, your world will mirror those beliefs and that thinking. If you believe the world is a dangerous place, you will experience danger. If you believe the universe is loving and supportive, you will experience your life as gentle, easy, and abundant. Our minds usually want to deny these truths and will go to any lengths to prove our limiting beliefs.

What limiting beliefs are you holding onto?

Is life hard or easy?

Do you have to work hard to get anywhere?

Is love safe and effortless or painful?

Is the world a safe or dangerous place?

How do you feel about the statement, "no pain no gain"?

Look at an area of your life where you are dissatisfied with the results you are getting. It could be your job, your relationship, your finances, or the way you feel about yourself. Write about it.

How does it feel?

What does this limitation say to you?

What do "they" think about this issue?

What did your parents tell you about this issue?

What does society think or believe about this issue?

What would you like to experience in your life instead?

Write several pages, write until you feel you are finished. Now put it away for a few days. Reread it at a later date, then condense it to a few paragraphs. Keep repeating the process until you have a few concise sentences that sum the whole thing up. Those are your beliefs about the issue. Change your beliefs to more positive ones and good results will follow. Our world is an accurate reflection of our beliefs.

MIRROR WORK

Our satisfaction lies in the journey,
not the destination.

My life seemed to be turning into a giant emotional roller coaster. One day I would be on top of the world, and the next day I would be too terrified to leave the house. At first I tried to ignore my emotions, but eventually I asked Miguel about them. He laughed and told me that I had brought a "friend" home with me during my meditation.

The ethereal realm is filled with beings that no longer have a body and have not yet gone back to the light. They feed on the emotions of other beings. The only way they know how to survive is to attach themselves to unsuspecting souls that wander across their path. Due to my studies, I spent a lot of time in their realms and they certainly seemed to love me. They scared me half to death. Now I realize that it was my fear that attracted them in the first place.

I would go into a meditation, and the next thing I knew I was afraid of my own shadow or severely depressed. Eventually I realized that whenever I felt that way, it was because one of those beings had again attached itself to me. I would go down to the temple, Miguel would laugh and send the being away. Miguel kept reassuring me that most of the time they are harmless, but I was not convinced. He would ask me why I let them bother me and I would get angry. I felt victimized by them. I certainly didn't feel like I had any control over them.

It often seemed as though Miguel and Sarita took a perverse pleasure in our terror over those creatures. One day two of my fellow apprentices were meditating in Miguel's yard. They began to feel uncomfortable, so they went inside. Once inside they became totally terrified. They were beside themselves with fear. Eventually Sister Sarita came home. She only tolerated Miguel's apprentices with amused indifference and now she looked disgusted. She began to yell in Spanish and to run around like she was crazy, which further terrified them. They were sure they were going to die. Then she started laughing. She told them not to conjure up beings unless they knew what to do with them. Then she opened the door and simply said, "out." To their amazement it left.

Eventually I realized that if I was to continue my studies, I had to learn how to tame these creatures. I had to stop allowing them to control me. I had to learn how to use them as allies as I journeyed into the other universes. Miguel stressed that on the physical plane we always had dominion, but if we allowed our fear to rule us, we could lose our lives when we were in their worlds. As a child I remember my father telling me that the only thing I had to fear was my fear. That really applied in this case. My fear actually invited these beings into my reality. Once my fear allowed them in, the door was open and they could follow me back home. For a time, most of my studies became a struggle to overcome my fears.

Before I started studying with Miguel, I was so out of touch with my emotions that I actually believed that I never felt fear. Miguel and the inorganic beings certainly dispelled that myth. As the Water Initiation approached, my emotional turmoil, as well as that of the group, seemed to escalate. Any unresolved emotional issues rose to the surface. I found myself losing my temper and crying a lot, things I had not done in years.

Miguel told us that it was time to prepare for our first initiation. He explained that each initiation was an opportunity for us to learn how to handle or channel more power. He said that it was very important to be as clear a channel as possible. Miguel reminded us that the path of a Nagual was very demanding. To achieve our freedom, we had to separate our emotions from our actions and now was the time to begin that process. He told us that this was a very important time in our studies, not only personally, but as a group. He said that we had to bond as a group and move beyond our fears. It was time for us to become a band or a ring of fire.

Miguel instructed us to pick out two times a day that the entire group could meditate. We were to meditate during those times as a group, although we would all be in separate places. Before we went into these meditations, we were to call upon our protector. Miguel told us that we would have to come into the temple and receive these protectors from him or Sarita. In the morning we were to do a normal meditation. In the evening we had to sit in a darkened room in front of a mirror, with a candle and a glass of water. We then were to do an open eye meditation. Miguel stressed that we were not to do these meditations until we received a protector.

A few days later I approached the temple with my usual sense of fear mixed with excitement. It was certainly a much friendlier place in the daylight. Miguel was late, as usual, so I went into the grocery store next door to the temple. They made the best carrot juice, so I ordered some and then settled down to enjoy it while I waited for Miguel. As I leaned against the building the sun felt so warm that I began to feel very drowsy. When I opened my eyes again Miguel was standing over me smiling.

We went into the temple. Even in the summer there was a slight chill in the air. He had brought along one of his assistants. We went into one of the healing rooms, and he motioned for me to sit on the table. He then instructed me to go into a meditative state. As I did he began to pray in Spanish. I began to sense a presence in the room, it was immense and felt powerful and loving. Miguel told me its name and explained it would be my protector as I explored the other realms. He also told me that I would have to ask for its help.

I thanked them and walked out into the afternoon sun. I felt lighter. I was hopeful that my protector could assist me in keeping some of my fear at bay. I was looking forward to the evening meditation. As the time approached I got everything ready. As soon as I sat down, I could feel the power of the group surround me. I began to see images on the wall behind me. I started to feel afraid, so I remembered to call upon my protector. The room immediately filled with his presence. I began to see strange images in the mirror. There were shadows on the wall behind me, but there was nothing in the room capable of making them. The shadows began to move and waver. My heart was pounding. Next my face began to change, blood began to come out of the corners of my eyes. Next I was looking at a face that I had never seen before. Then the mirror went blank. I decided that it was time to end the meditation.

That night my dreams were very strange, but when I awoke I was unable to remember any of them clearly. I was almost afraid to look at myself in the mirror as I washed my face the next morning. I nervously sat down for the morning meditation.

As soon as I closed my eyes, I could feel the presence of the group. I immediately went into a very deep meditation. I found myself flying. I could feel the muscles in my shoulders adjusting the position of my wings. My fingers began to move so I could catch the wind currents better. I had become an eagle. I wasn't imagining that I was an eagle, I was actually an eagle. I found myself circling in the sky, I felt so free. I was elated. For a long time I enjoyed flying along, occasionally taking advantage of a thermal current to rise higher. I was extremely alert and aware of everything happening on the ground below me. I was constantly scanning the horizon. I flew with my head down, turning my head from side to side watching for movement of any kind.

I saw a blur of movement off to my right. I found myself diving towards a rabbit. In the back of my mind I thought "Oh no, I am going to kill a rabbit." As the scene unfolded it seemed perfectly natural. I knew that it was correct. I knew that I would eat this animal. I flew downward at a tremendous speed, the feeling of power was almost overwhelming. At the last moment I turned and grabbed the rabbit in my talons. I had to adjust my wings to accommodate the additional weight. The rabbit offered up its spirit to me, so I received the gift of its energy gratefully. I flew to my cliff overlooking the valley. I let out a piercing cry of thanks and began to eat the rabbit.

Gradually I found myself seated back in my living room. It took me quite a while to adjust to being in my body again. I was anxious to go to class later that week. I wanted to know what was happening to me. The next few nights the meditations continued to be bizarre. I continued to see one face after another in the mirror. Some of the faces were men and some were women, some young and some old. Many of them seemed to be in a great deal of emotional pain and fear.

As I watched this procession of faces I began to see a pattern. Each of these characters had on a mask. Even though they were feeling fearful, angry, or sad on the inside they all put on a brave face. I began to realize that most of my life I had done the same thing. No matter what was going on inside, I always said I was fine. I seldom let anyone know my true feelings. I always carried my pain inside and seldom even acknowledged it to myself. No wonder I had been so fearful lately. All those years of stored emotions were beginning to surface.

Each night as I meditated the flood gates opened up. I saw years of rage and sadness come to the surface. Much of it dissolved, some of it I was unable to let go of yet. After several days of this, I was really looking forward to class.

When I arrived at the temple, several of the students were already waiting outside. As we nervously compared notes, I realized we all had similar experiences. The faces or images were different, but the results were the same. Any buried thoughts or feelings were coming to the surface. The size of the class that night was slightly smaller than usual. Miguel arrived and we slowly began to file in.

He started the class by asking us to share our experiences during the meditations. When I shared about becoming an eagle and eating a rabbit, one of the other students became very agitated. She shared that she had become a rabbit. Many of the other students had also assumed their animal forms. Many of them had also seen bizarre images in the mirror. Miguel said that it was important for us to release as much of the past as possible before we attended the Water Initiation.

Miguel would not tell us much about the initiation itself, but he began to explain why it was so important to clear out the past. One of the dangers of handling power is that it was a relentless task master. As we handled more energy, anything unlike the light would rise to the surface. If we enjoyed manipulating others, we would be tempted by the dark side of the energy to use manipulation. Our thoughts would manifest much more rapidly. The more loving we were, the easier the process would be. If we focused on anger, we would pull anger towards ourselves. It was very important to be gentle and loving with ourselves.

Miguel went on to say that the greatest enemy of a spiritual warrior, besides old age, was the lure of power. Power was very seductive. It was very important for us to always check our motives or we could be lost. Lost to what, he would never say.

As I drove home that night I began to muse about Miguel's warning. What had he really meant? I turned off the freeway towards the beach and I was struck by the beauty of all the street lights. They looked like the twinkling lights I had seen in my meditation. Fear began to rise up in my body, and I realized that most of my life I assumed that the world was a hostile place. I feared that "they" were out to get me. Now I was studying with this Mexican Nagual who was telling me I could be lost. I started to get angry, but then I remembered that feeling of peace I had when I was in my meditation viewing the world as energy.

Slowly I began to remember that Miguel said that this energy had consciousness and that the consciousness was one of love. I began to think about Sister Sarita. She was a very loving soul. As a young woman she had been diagnosed with cancer. In those days cancer was a painful death sentence. She went to a spiritual healing center in Mexico City, and she was cured. After that, Sarita dedicated her life to becoming a healer and helping others. Sarita had an almost childlike faith in a very loving universal energy, a God that really cared about everyone.

I began comparing my beliefs in a punishing universe with her loving universe. I could see why I was afraid all the time. I decided that it was time for me to change some of my beliefs. Perhaps it was time for me to believe in a universe that was *for* me, rather than against me. That simple shift in my conscious-ness changed almost everything. My visions in the mirror were much friendlier. Even the inorganic beings seemed less hostile after that. I slept more soundly than I had in years.

The next morning I awoke early feeling excited about doing the morning meditation. As soon as I sat down in my chair I could feel the presence of the group. I immediately went into a deep meditation. I was surrounded by an energy that was incredibly loving. I had never felt anything like it. The energy was so gentle and warm. I could feel my heart slowly opening and softening. The only way I can describe the experience was that I was in the presence of God. The energy just tenderly enfolded me and held me. I had never experienced such love and gentleness. Tears welled up in my eyes, and I felt years of sadness and loneliness melt away. As I explored this energy, I found that it was also amazingly powerful. I felt totally safe and protected and loved, so very loved. I knew that I was accepted just the way I was. I did not want to return from that meditation.

The evening meditations became more of a process of discovery and release. I saw images from my childhood. Old wounds that I had consciously forgotten about came up to the surface, and I was able to forgive myself and my parents. I began to have that unconditional love for myself and my world. It was a miracle, most of the time I felt wonderful. Occasionally my mind would step in, and I would forget everything and be stuck in fear and negativity again. I kept returning to the love. Whenever I remembered to, I would ask that energy I met in that morning meditation to love me and it would.

A few weeks later, Miguel announced that the Water Initiation would take place the following week. Everyone nervously asked what we should do to prepare ourselves. Should we fast, should we…? He just smiled, told us to wear all white, and to be here the following week.

EXERCISE SIX

Meditation is a wonderful gift that can affect all levels of our being. If you don't already meditate on a daily basis, try it for a while and observe what a difference it makes in your life. Find a place to get quiet and make sure you won't be disturbed for ten to fifteen minutes. Begin by relaxing your body and focusing your attention on your breathing.

Next focus your attention on your heart. Let your mind become quiet, allow your thoughts to flow through you, and begin to "think" through your heart. Take time and practice listening to your heart.

Your heart's voice is always loving and kind. It makes you feel good when you listen to it. If the voice you hear is harsh or suggests strange things, it is your mind. In your heart resides an intelligent, loving, and wise energy that can help you transform your life if you learn to listen to it. Your heart is your spiritual center—your sacred self.

Your heart will guide you lovingly on your path if you listen. Notice how different you feel when you listen to your heart instead of your mind. The difference is usually quite dramatic. When I listen to my head, I feel stress. When I listen to my heart, I feel at peace. Choose to listen to your heart.

Often we will go to any length to avoid quiet time or time spent alone. If you are having resistance or if you are having difficulty finding time to meditate, become an observer for a few days. Notice what you say to yourself.

What scares you the most about spending quiet time with yourself?

What excuses do you give yourself for not finding time to meditate?

How does you mind talk to you?

Is your mind friendly and supportive or critical?

Does your mind encourage you to continue on your spiritual path or does it tell you it is a waste of time?

Practice going into your heart and listening. How does your heart talk to you? Is it gentle or harsh?

What sort of things does it tell you?

Often your heart will give you common sense information that you already know; information that would improve the quality of your life if you would just apply it. Listen to the loving voice of your heart, it will make your journey much easier and your life will be much more enjoyable.

7

THE WATER INITIATION

*Our answers can only come
if we are willing to listen.*

 As the day of the initiation approached, I found myself
feeling nervous as well as excited. I decided I needed
just the right outfit for the initiation. I was very upset that I
couldn't find whites that matched. I was amazed by the number
of shades of white available. If Miguel had been aware of my
dilemma, I am sure he would have laughed. He had said to prepare for our initiation in any way that seemed appropriate. I
decided to have a channeling session done by one of my friends.

The session was quite interesting. The entity spoke about
initiations and their significance. He told me stories about the
ancients and how the priests and leaders of the tribe would
always go through some sort of an initiation to prepare themselves for their duties. The initiates would be changed physically as well as mentally by the ceremony.

The basis of most initiations is spiritual in nature. The initiates would be put into some sort of altered state in which they would have a vision. Afterwards they would usually have a stronger connection with their concept of God and would often feel a sense of personal guidance from that energy.

He also talked about the initiations in ancient Egypt. The teachers in Egypt would administer drugs to the initiates. These drugs would take them to the verge of death where they would have to face their demons. If they had learned well, and the gods were pleased with them, they would live. If not, they would go to the land of the dead to wander for centuries until their souls could be restored.

Those altered states were fact-finding missions. The initiates would come back wiser or die in the process. Initiations in the past were very serious matters, they were a commitment to a certain path. The entity went on to say that modern man had lost the significance of initiations, as well as the power generated by them. He talked about the beauty of the Catholic Mass and what a powerful ceremony it was. He went on to say that the church had forgotten the true significance of the mass. The priest's actual function was to physically channel the energy of God. Any ceremony can be an act of power if we allow it to be. Our lives can become sacred acts. Our entire lives are sacred, we have just forgotten the sanctity of life.

At the end of the session, I put on my white outfit and drove down to the temple. When I pulled up out front it looked like a Good Humor Man convention. We all looked rather conspicuous walking down the streets dressed all in white. I was very surprised to find Miguel already in the temple. The altar had fresh flowers on it and Sister Sarita was sitting in front of it. She was radiant. Her husband and her older son sat beside her. They were all people of great power. There were also several people there I didn't recognize. Eventually I found out they were part of Sister Sarita's original group of apprentices.

We all stood around nervously, my stomach was all tied up in knots. Everyone was strangely quiet. The temple felt so different. Usually things were informal, but tonight the air was electric. Next to Sarita was a table with a beautiful abalone shell on it. The shell was filled with water and beautiful pink rose petals were floating on the surface. As I looked around the temple that night, it felt magical. Miguel told us to remain standing and that we would be told where to sit. He also told us we could ask the universe for a request when we came up to the altar. Miguel also suggested we give some serious thought to our commitment.

Eventually we were all told where to sit, and we went into a meditation. Sarita went into a trance, then she began to speak. Slowly in Spanish she began by blessing the group and calling upon the power of God to be there with us. As she invoked the various powers, you could feel the energy in the room building. Whenever she did her healing work she was in a trance. She called it putting on her protector.

Once Sarita put on her protector, she stood up again. The people around her stood up as well, and they also blessed the group and assisted in building up the energy in the room. The energy in the air was so thick it felt almost overwhelming. I was relieved when the ceremony began.

Slowly I opened my eyes and adjusted to being back in the room. I had been unable to go into a deep meditation because of my excitement and curiosity. Sister Sarita stood in front of the altar surrounded by all of her helpers. The scene looked very surreal. The flowers were so vivid and the people around Sarita seemed to exude an aura of love. I had never seen auras before, but that night I could. The people were radiant. They all looked so gentle and kind. They were all in a trance. Standing beside Sarita was a woman who frequently translated for her.

One by one, Miguel lead his apprentices up to the altar and had them stand before Sister Sarita. He would place her hand on their heads and their ceremony would begin. She would start by blessing them and then tell them about their path. She would ask them if they had a wish and what they were dedicating themselves to. The whole ceremony had a gentle and private quality to it. As people returned to their seats their eyes had a faraway look in them. Most of them looked stunned.

Miguel came for me. I approached the altar with a bit of hesitancy. Did I really want to dedicate myself to this path? Did I really have a choice? I thought not. At that instant I felt truly guided. I saw how so many times destiny had seemingly intervened and led me to this very moment. Whenever I saw Sarita she always welcomed me warmly and gave me a big hug. Then she would immediately began to talk rapidly to me in Spanish. I had always wished for a translator, tonight I had one.

Sarita placed her hand on my head. I bowed my head, and she began to pour water from the abalone shell over me. The fragrance of roses lingered. Then slowly she began to speak. She blessed me and thanked the Father for bringing me to her. She said that I was a great healer and teacher. She said that I was destined to carry my message to many. At times Sarita said that my path might feel heavy, and she asked for guidance so that I would not to loose my way. As she spoke I felt my consciousness shifting. I felt myself slipping into another reality. I was seeing what she was saying before I heard the words. I was seeing images of myself before large groups of people talking with a sense of ease. I found that hard to believe, I hated talking in front of people.

Sarita had me kneel down in front of her and she held both of my hands. She asked the Father to bless my hands for the healings they would do. She put her hands on my head and asked for a blessing for the knowledge that I would share. Then she looked upwards and asked the heavens to provide for my needs and to make my path easy. She placed her hands over my heart and asked that my heart always remain open so I could share my love with those in need. She asked me if I had a request. I stood there stunned for a moment, and then I asked for the ability to do whatever was necessary. Miguel led me back to my seat and I sat there amazed. I felt a warm glow growing within me so I settled back to enjoy it. I was lost in thought.

When I lived in Vermont, I saw a massage therapist on a weekly basis. I remember one day asking her where she lived in her body. She looked at me very strangely. I was trying to figure out where my consciousness resided in my body. Most of my life I had lived totally in my head. I usually tried to intellectualize things rather than feel or experience them. As I sat there that night, I realized that for once my consciousness was in my heart. I could really feel, and as I looked around the room I could easily sense what others were feeling. It was a strange sensation. My attention slowly began to focus on the ceremony again.

After the last apprentice was finished, Sarita did a consecration ceremony for several people who had been studying with her for a long time. It was a simple, yet beautiful ceremony in which she blessed their paths and made them holy people, teachers, or priests. I could feel the love flowing around her. The people she blessed began to glow and a lovely peace came over them. After the consecration she slumped over and was led back to her chair. A few moments later she came out of the trance, looked around, and smiled. She said a short closing prayer in which she thanked the Father and all his helpers for being there. She asked that all those who had participated that day be blessed as well. Then Sarita motioned for us to begin feasting.

The change in mood was dramatic. One moment everyone was serious and solemn, the next moment everyone was laughing and joking. The table was so colorful. I had barely noticed it when I came in, but it certainly was a drastic contrast to everyone around the table dressed in white. The food looked wonderful and smelled delicious. As I looked around at the crowd, I felt a strange mixture of emotions. I felt a sense of belonging, while at the same time I felt like an outsider. Someone brought Sarita a plate of food to where she sat in the corner.

I stood there and watched her for a while. She was an amazing lady. Sarita always looked very regal, yet everything about her was very humble. She always appeared to be holding court. For a woman in her late seventies, she was incredibly spry and agile. If someone hadn't told me her age, I would have guessed that she was in her late fifties or early sixties. She noticed me watching her and smiled at me, then she motioned for me to come over. She gave me a big hug and held my hands. She nodded and smiled. At that moment I felt very loved and I wished that there wasn't a language barrier. I thanked her and she gave me a warm hug. She said something briefly in Spanish and then she turned to talk to someone else.

I wandered over towards Miguel. He was smiling broadly and gave me an affectionate hug. I had learned to be wary of him when he did that because he would often push on my power points and I would find myself off somewhere else. As if he had read my thoughts, he smiled at me and said not tonight. Everyone was very animated. No one mentioned the ceremony. I was feeling tired, so I said my goodbyes.

As I walked out into the night air, the world felt different. I looked up at the night sky and saw a sliver of moon and all those twinkling stars. I felt like I was part of the universe. The night seemed strangely quiet. I could smell the ocean and I decided to go down to the beach for a walk. I drove down to the ocean and went for a stroll along the boardwalk. I loved sitting on the sea wall watching the waves reflect the lights of the city. The sound was incredibly hypnotic, I truly felt at peace and loved. I realized that the quiet was coming from my head, for once my mind wasn't analyzing everything, I was just enjoying the moment.

I drove home and took a long hot bath. The water felt so sensual. My dog stuck her head over the edge of the tub to get petted, her fur felt so smooth. I looked at her and saw the love she had for me. I was experiencing everything much more intensely. It was as if someone had turned up the volume on my senses. It was eerie and exciting. When I fell asleep, I dreamed about events and people that made no sense at the time. I have since lived some of the dreams. In the morning my world was back to normal.

EXERCISE SEVEN

Rituals are wonderful experiences. I find it sad that our culture doesn't use them more often. You can create one for yourself. Find a place that is special to you, perhaps invite some friends. Create a ritual that has meaning to the essence of who you are.

You might try going to various churches and observe their rituals. Go to a Buddhist temple or a Jewish synagog and just watch the ceremony. Go to as many different churches as you can with an open mind and watch with your heart.

If you have the opportunity to attend any Native American rituals, by all means do so. When you observe rituals, it is important to allow yourself to feel them rather than merely observe them with your mind. There can be a great deal of power and love in a ceremony. Allow yourself to feel it.

If you decide to create a ritual for yourself, make sure each element of it is meaningful to you. A friend of mine wanted to let go of an old lover, so she decided to do a ritual. First she wrote a farewell letter. In it she said everything she wanted or needed to say about the past and how she felt. Then she said goodbye and set this person free. She went down to the ocean and built a small fire. She read the letter out loud to the universe, then burned it. Afterwards she felt much freer. Some people tie letters or messages to balloons and release them. If you use a balloon, honor Mother Earth by using a biodegradable one.

Another way to get in touch with the power of ceremony is to go out in nature. Really allow yourself to feel nature, become a student or initiate of the elements by just allowing yourself to feel them. Ask nature to teach you and then sit still long enough to listen for the answer.

Make your entire life a sacred act. Practice blessing yourself, your life, your friends, and your food. Saying a blessing before a meal is a type of ceremony.

How would you define a ceremony or ritual?

When you think about initiations, what kinds of mental images do you have?

What were you told about rituals as a child?

How do you feel about rituals? Are they sacred or foolish?

What is your definition of sacred?

What is sacred in your life?

Watch a ceremony of an indigenous tribe. How does it feel?

8

HABITS AND ROUTINES

*In our attempt to control things,
we are often controlled by them.*

 When I woke up the next morning, I felt like the night before had all been a bizarre dream. As I moved around my apartment getting ready for work, I felt a strange sense of loss. I sat down to meditate and the only thing I could get in touch with was an intense feeling of restlessness. I always enjoyed seeing the sunrise on my way to work, but as I drove to work that morning and watched the sun rise over the mountains it looked strangely flat. I went through my morning feeling like a robot. Luckily I only worked until noon.

As I sat in the parking lot, I felt tears welling up in my eyes. I sat there and wept silently. I started the car and found myself driving to the barrio. I felt so much better once I saw those huge painted figures on the freeway columns. As I approached the temple, I was relieved to see that the door was open. As my eyes adjusted to the darkness, I saw Miguel sitting behind the desk smiling at me. He looked as though he had been waiting for me. He came around the desk and gave me a warm hug.

We went into one of the healing rooms and began to talk. I told him how I had been feeling all day. He smiled and began to explain to me what had happened energetically to me. He pulled out the white board and drew the following diagram.

INITIATION

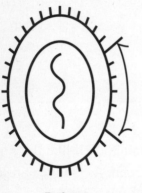

Before   After

Notice that in the **After** illustration the door is wide open and the security point has expanded.

FIGURE 8-1

Miguel said that one of the purposes of an initiation was to open the initiates' security point so they could receive more of the ethereal energy. Last night he said I had been very willing, so when Sarita did my ceremony my security point had been blown wide open. Energetically I was no longer the same person who had come to the temple last night. In a sense I no longer fit into my old life. That life belonged to the old me.

My first reaction was "Oh, great now what?" Miguel suggested we go for a walk. One of his favorite places to walk was a park nestled against the ocean. It was a very peaceful place, with tree lined walkways bordering the ocean. On the drive over to the park, Miguel was strangely silent. As we walked along he began to talk about doorways to the ethereal worlds. I was no longer the old Susan, so who was I? That search for the true self was one of the major challenges of the spiritual warrior, we had to remember who and what we truly are.

At that point we were walking past a tree. He stopped and told me to climb it. I felt somewhat foolish as I tried to scamper up the tree. I hadn't done that for years, so at first I felt very awkward. After I had a climbed for a while, he told me to find a comfortable place to sit. I settled down in the crotch of some tree branches. I immediately began to sense the energy of the tree. The energy began to flow through me. It was a very peaceful energy. I had a sense of patience and a feeling of just being. There was absolutely no struggle or disharmony in its energy. It felt good and it certainly was quite a contrast to my energy.

Next Miguel told me to focus my attention on the ocean. There was a soft breeze and the waves were gently lapping against the shore. The sun was already beginning to get lower in the sky, the water sparkled and danced in a ribbon of light. Miguel instructed me to focus my attention on the shadows in the water. As I did, he reminded me that it was the habit of human beings to focus their attention on the bright parts of life. We seldom look at the shadows, yet the shadows are what give our lives definition.

As he spoke I felt a gentle pulling on my very being. I felt a doorway open and in the distance I heard Miguel's voice telling me to remain in both places. I was aware of myself in the tree, and I was also walking through a crack in the ocean. Whenever I entered one of these worlds, I had a sense of being tilted and of my body rocking back and forth. I also felt a tingle of fear just before I would step through the crack. As I stood in the crack, or doorway, I felt as if the two worlds were superimposed on each other and neither one was real. I felt disoriented. I again heard Miguel's voice off in the distance, telling me to relax and to stay in both places. His voice sounded like it was coming from the bottom of a barrel filled with water.

The beings in this reality were very loving and playful. At first they ignored my presence, but then they began to look at me curiously. I knew they were communicating with one another, but I was uncertain about what they were saying. I could feel their love and kindness though. I had a sense that they could teach me how to be happier. In that instant I knew that love was the only thing that was real, everything else was a creation of my mind. I felt like I was in an educational cartoon. If I would relax, not take life seriously, and act in a loving way, life would be grand. Drama was only useful as amusement for my mind. I saw how all of my beliefs and my need to understand and struggle was totally unnecessary. If I saw myself as a fictional character, I could have fun and enjoy the game of life. I could let go of my mind and be free.

I took a deep breath and was again sitting in the tree. I was puzzled because I was uncertain how I knew all of that. Miguel told me to focus my attention on the shadows in the tree. He told me to look at the dark places and ignore the light. As I did, I felt the presence of an immense being that was very benevolent. When I focused on the sparkling bright leaves, it was gone.

I was curious. When I looked down Miguel was walking away, so I climbed down the tree and began to follow him. We walked along in silence for a while. I began to think about what had just happened, and I realized that my experience of life was severely limited by my habit of focusing my attention on the bright spots. I realized that my focus generally tended to be superficial. As I began to generalize that thought, I saw how limited my view of life had been. I wondered if I could apply the concept of shadows to the shadowy emotions in life as well. All those feelings, like sadness, anger, and jealousy, were the ones I was not proud of. They were the feelings I tried to avoid. I began to see how the concept of shadows could apply to many areas in my life. I was amazed. When I looked at Miguel, he was smiling broadly at me, nodding his head in approval. I wondered how he did it, so often he seemed to be reading my mind.

As we drove back to the temple, Miguel told me that even sounds had shadows. Without our shadows we would cease to exist. Without evil we would not have good, without darkness there would be no light. Miguel suggested that I explore shadows for a while. I had a lot of food for thought as I drove home from the temple that day. On the way home I tried listening for the shadows in sound, without much luck.

The next morning I got up for work before dawn as usual. The morning was always very special to me. The place where I took my dog for a walk overlooked the mountains as well as the ocean. The sky was just beginning to turn pink and the birds were starting to sing. As I walked along with my dog that morn-ing, I began to hear the shadows in the birds' songs. It was mag-ical, the silence between their notes was more beautiful then any music I had ever heard. I was elated. I stood there in total awe as I listened to the pauses between the sounds. It felt as if an entire universe existed in those pauses.

That afternoon as I went for a walk on the beach, I began to play with my shadow. At first I just watched my shadow as I walked along the sand. The longer I watched, the stronger the feeling of being watched became. After a while it was a strange feeling, I wasn't sure who was watching who. It was late after-noon and my shadow was immense. I could feel a definite pres-ence in my shadow. I wasn't sure whether it was friendly or not. I tried to communicate with it, but I didn't have much success. As soon as I decided the presence was benevolent, I returned home.

I drove to class that week with a wonderful feeling of antic-ipation and elation. I was surprised, the class had dwindled to about half of its original size. Miguel greeted everyone, then began talking about habits and routines. Our initiation had dis-solved many of the illusions we had created about our lives. One of the illusions we had lost was the sense of normalcy and safety we usually received from our routines. In a sense it had rearranged the way we felt about many of them. Overnight we had changed drastically, so we no longer felt comfortable with the way we had been living.

Usually our routines change slowly, over time. When we start a new job or relationship everything is unfamiliar. It takes time before we establish new and familiar patterns. Some people love routines, other people rapidly become bored with them.

They are all part of our mind's defense of its security point. Whether we feel safer with routines or without them is just another part of our routines or habitual way of acting and reacting. In a real sense we are all robots. We seldom freely choose our behaviors, we merely act in the same way over and over.

Miguel told us that routines were dangerous to a spiritual warrior for many reasons. As long as our life is ruled by routines, we aren't free. We are not choosing our behaviors. Our emotions and actions are still linked together. Our minds feel safe when we are acting like robots because then they know that action A will always follow action B. Our minds work exactly like computers; garbage in—garbage out. Once a computer is programmed, the only choice is to follow the rules of that program. If we try to do things differently, the computer doesn't respond. We can reprogram our minds though. However we can't reprogram our minds with our minds. We must do our reprogramming from the ethereal or spiritual level.

Miguel said that the initiation had given each of us the opportunity to access the ethereal and spiritual levels in a very profound manner. We could use that opening to change many of our behaviors, or we could fight to stay the same. We were no longer students. Miguel explained that we were now hunters. As hunters we had to be aware, remain patient, have perseverance, and observe the routines. He said that we no longer had the luxury of going through our lives being unconscious. We had to wake up. Handling power carried with it certain responsibilities, and one of those was awareness.

He suggested that we begin to consciously change our routines. If we always go to work at a certain time and use a certain route, change it. If we always get out of bed on the left side, get up on the right side. He told us to do as many things as possible differently. Eat with a different hand, get dressed, then brush our teeth, put our clothes on in a different order, eat at different times, etc. By doing this we would continue to open up our security point and let in more ethereal energy so we could change more easily. Our minds always want to maintain our routines so everything can remain the same. By changing the routines we can reprogram our minds.

He went on to say that habits were routines to which we had a strong emotional attachment. Habits were routines we were addicted to repeating. They usually served some sort of an emotional purpose. In order to change habits, we had to access our spiritual energies. We also had to find new ways to meet the emotional needs that fuel our addiction to those habits. Routines are easy to change, we merely have to decide to change them. Habits are much more deeply ingrained and require a decision and a willingness to access our spiritual core. As we begin to change habits and routines, our emotional baggage rises to the surface of our minds. Frequently, as soon as we become uncomfortable, we go back to our old behaviors. As hunters we need to observe those behaviors and begin to break free of them.

After a short break we began our meditation. I was in the outer circle, and I could feel Miguel begin to work in power points. I felt like the top of my head was about to blow off. The next instant I felt myself floating in space. I was looking at myself and I saw myself as pure energy. I felt an incredible sense of oneness and peace. I saw filaments running throughout my body, some were smooth and sparkling, while others were very twisted and knotted. I realized that some of the twisted ones were my habits and routines. I began to gently unwrap some of them. As I did I knew my behaviors were also changing. Each time I untwisted one, I felt lighter and freer. I could tug on a fiber and immediately know what it represented. Some were loving and free, while others were confining and angry. The angry filaments felt hot and rough. Each one had a different feeling, texture, and meaning. My entire personality was a mass of fibers sitting there in front of me. I could choose to rearrange them any way I wanted. Off in the distance I heard Miguel calling us back.

That next week I practiced changing some of my routines. It was fun, exciting, and made everything seem new. I noticed that when I made conscious choices rather than just automatically doing things, I began to feel more alive. It was amazing. I felt like I was waking up from a long nap.

The place where I worked sold meditation tapes. I listened to one in which you went into a deep meditation and then began to focus on your individual senses. After you were totally relaxed, the tape had you open your eyes slightly and say, "I see." Then you mentally listed all the objects and noticed all the details of anything in your line of sight. Next you focused on your hearing, then smell, touch, and taste. The next day when I took my dog for a walk, I could hear and smell someone cutting the grass several blocks away. The volume on my senses had been turned up several notches. Everything looked brighter, smelled better, and sounded wonderful.

Between changing my routines and doing that meditation, my experience of life really seemed to intensify. I never knew I could feel so alive, I hadn't realized that I had anesthetized myself so much. I began to understand at a much greater depth what Miguel meant by personal freedom.

EXERCISE EIGHT

Find a place in nature and observe the shadows. Focus on the dark areas and see what you sense and feel. Trees and water are excellent subjects. Just breathe deeply and concentrate on the shadows until you feel a shift in your consciousness. Stand in the sun for a few moments and then step into the shadows.

What do you feel or sense? Naturally it will be cooler, but what changes besides the temperature?

Practice listening to the "shadows" or quiet places in sounds. Listen to a bird sing and listen to the shadows. There is an amazing world that we seldom acknowledge that exists between the sounds. The phrase "pregnant pause" is a very good way to describe the spaces between the sounds. Those spaces are composed of an entire world beyond our normal perspective. Allow yourself to begin exploring this world.

The shadows in the physical world are wonderful to explore, but the shadows within ourselves are the very things that limit our experience of life. As we explore our emotional shadows our life is transformed. The shadowy parts of ourselves are the parts we deny, dislike, or avoid for some reason.

Do you avoid your anger, sadness, or neediness? Why?

What emotions do you avoid?

How does avoiding these emotions serve you?

Do you avoid confrontations? Why?

Do you avoid intimacy? Why?

Are you doing what you love for a living?

How do the emotions you avoid affect your life?

What shadows do you have in your past?

List your secrets.

How do your secrets serve you?

How do your secrets restrict you?

Are you willing to release them?

Take some time and think about your shadow. Define it for yourself. Write about what you hold within your shadow. Think about how upset Peter Pan was when he lost his shadow.

Go for a walk in nature early in the morning or late in the afternoon so your shadow will be at its longest. How does it feel?

Observe your shadow. Are you watching it or is it watching you?

THE KNOWN AND THE UNKNOWABLE

*We are always free to choose,
but only after we know that we are free to choose.*

At times it seemed as though the longer I studied with Miguel the less I was certain about. My old ideas and beliefs I held about how the world operated and what life was about no longer seemed to make any sense. I grew up with a belief that a successful life was one in which you achieved financial stability, and when you were 65 years old you retired. Then, if you were lucky, you began to enjoy life. I always believed my happiness came from an external source and that if I worked really hard today, I might get to be happy tomorrow. The problem was tomorrow never came, and if my happiness came from something outside of myself, it could easily be taken away.

One day Miguel's car was stolen. He was totally neutral about the event. A few days later he said the theft had really been good luck for him. Without the car payments he was able to qualify for a loan on a house. I was baffled. If my car had been stolen, insured or not, it would have been a good excuse for some high drama in my life. I would have at least used the theft to beat myself up about why I had pulled the event into my life in the first place. I might have concluded that my poverty consciousness or my fear of loss had caused my car to be stolen. When I asked Miguel, he just said someone wanted his car more then he did. I asked him if he had any attachment to anything physical. He said the only thing he was still attached to was his children and he was trying to let go of them as well.

At first I felt confused and angered by his responses. I felt he was being apathetical. A short while later, my apartment was broken into and I was extremely upset. They had stolen all my jewelry. Eventually I concluded that I was still attached to feeling like a victim. When I told Miguel about my theft, he just reminded me that they wanted my jewelry more then I did. He asked me what purpose my attachment served. I realized my attachment to the jewelry was the real cause of my emotional upset, not the theft itself. He asked me why I had bought the jewelry. I told him I bought it because it made me happy.

As I began to think about the whole event, I realized that the jewelry had served its purpose. It had pleased me to buy and wear it. Now I could continue to put my attention on the loss and remain miserable, or I could focus my attention on the pleasure it had brought me. The choice was mine, and it depended on my intentions as well as where I put my attention. Was my intention to be happy or to feel like a victim?

I suddenly remembered a conversation Miguel and I had about the "old ones." The old ones Miguel referred to were the

Naguals of the past. They were amazing wizards and shape shifters. They were able to place their entire essence or spirit into an inanimate object. I was told that they were from the old school. When I asked what that meant, he smiled and told me to be glad I wasn't an apprentice then.

In the old days Naguals had been both revered and feared by their people. There was a great deal of competition, and Naguals often fought among themselves, trying to steal each other's power. They believed that they were in competition with the universe, as well as each other. Consequently there was very little love and acceptance in their lives. The old ones tended to be harsh and dogmatic.

In those days they perceived the universe to be a great eagle that consumed your spirit when you died. They believed that humans were food for the eagle, so when you died you ceased to exist. That was what they perceived when they had journeyed to the other world. As Miguel put it "they had caught the energy wrong." Whatever information people receive on the ethereal must be translated by their minds and often the information is misinterpreted. The old ones spent a great deal of time trying to understand the unknowable. They were constantly looking for a way to prevent themselves from being consumed and losing their identities at death.

Rather then placing their attention on things they could change, they focused their attention on things beyond their control. Miguel told me that it was very important to focus only on the knowable or you wasted a lot of time and energy. He defined the knowable as things that we could easily understand and control in some way. He went on to say that it was equally important to understand our intentions or the reasons we wanted to control something.

He said that the old ones had become so obsessed with defeating death that they were unable to focus on anything else. They lost themselves in a search that had no end. They had used their power to learn how to place their consciousness in objects. This skill didn't move them any closer to their personal freedom. They had forgotten their original purpose or intention. In a sense they were caught up in a vicious cycle of seeking and never finding. The more they searched, the further they moved from their spiritual center.

They had lost sight of their true goals and intentions. The old ones had forgotten that life was a search for harmony with the earth and themselves. As Naguals their task was to lead their people into a greater awareness of their spiritual nature. Instead they decided to try to defeat the universe. They were unable or unwilling to surrender their will. They were warriors first, spiritual beings second. They placed all their attention on winning in the physical realm rather then exploring their spiritual nature.

When a fish is removed from water, no matter how hard it tries to breathe the air, it suffocates because water is its element. We are spiritual beings and no matter how hard we try focusing on this reality alone, it is not enough to sustain us. We have to grow spiritually as well. The old ones had become so proficient at manipulating the physical world that they wanted to live forever. Instead once they transferred their consciousness into an inanimate object when their bodies died, they became trapped in the illusion of this reality. They were no longer free to control their reality and became trapped in those inanimate objects.

As my studies continued, I began to realize that one of the dangers in studying in this tradition was losing one's way. So much emphasis was placed on controlling this reality that it was easy to forget my original intentions. The power was very seductive. I began to realize how important my intentions really were. Why was I studying with Miguel anyway? At first it was a matter of curiosity, then I wanted my life to get better. I wanted to be happy and I had a very limited definition of happiness. My belief that my happiness resided outside of myself still lingered, I still thought more money, a place on the beach, and the perfect relationship would "make me feel better." I now know that those things are nice to have, but I feel better because of what I tell myself, not because I have those things. My happiness is a matter of my perception.

I became concerned about my intentions. I expressed those concerns to Miguel and he said that it was time for the students to go to the mountains for a weekend. I was anxiously anticipating the trip up to the mountains for the weekend. I hadn't seen snow since I left Vermont and I didn't miss it one bit. We met at the temple and started off for the mountains. After a few wrong turns we found the cabin. By the time we got there it was dark. It was freezing, but the stars were magical.

We started a fire in the fireplace, then Miguel had us sit outside and look at our reflections in the sliding glass doors by candlelight. The air was still and the flame from the candle barely wavered. I hadn't been that cold in years. It took me a few minutes to stop my teeth from chattering, but after a short while I was able to drift into a light meditative state. It was the first time I had done an open eye meditation with a group. As I looked at the glass I saw everyone's animal form. It was fascinating. For the first time I could see the other people change forms as well as myself. The air was still and the power of the group was slowly growing.

Suddenly a strong wind came up and blew out the candle. Everyone was jolted back to this reality and looked very startled. The fire was beginning to take the chill off the cabin so we all curled up in front of the fireplace. Miguel smiled broadly. I had really expected him to begin telling horrible ghost stories, but instead he yawned and said it was time to go to sleep.

I awoke very early the next morning with a tremendous amount of pain in my eye. It was running and very sore. I was in the bathroom putting cold water on it when Miguel came in. For a brief moment he looked concerned, but then he asked me what I had done to my eye. I wanted to kill him or at least say, "You fool, can't you see I am in pain?" He motioned for me to follow him outside. He put his hand on my eye and told me to relax. One of the other students began to work on it as well and the pain eased. Before I knew it, my eye had stopped running. Miguel and I went outside for a walk before the others woke up.

The day was bright and clear. I could already feel the warmth of the sun. We began to walk along an old fire trail. After being in the city, the mountain air seemed so crisp and clean. It was peaceful and tranquil as we walked along.

We stopped in front of a tree and Miguel told me to focus my attention on a squirrel that was nervously watching us. Slowly, as I focused my attention on the squirrel, I could feel a presence standing behind me. I looked at Miguel and he told me that the being was my protector. He told me to allow my consciousness to follow my attention. Suddenly I could feel myself sitting on the branch looking back at myself. I was startled. I immediately found myself standing beside Miguel again.

Miguel told me to try again. Slowly I found myself inside the squirrel's body again. I began to notice how differently he used his senses. His whole perception of reality was different than mine. He was watching us intently. As long as his attention was focused on us, he felt in control. I am not sure if control is the right word, but he knew he could react appropriately. The squirrel felt safe, he knew he could rapidly escape. As I began to explore his body and senses, he noticed me and began to scamper off. He jumped into the next tree and scolded me loudly, as if to say, "Stay out of my body." I had invaded his territory and he wasn't used to that. I laughed at his indignation.

Miguel told me I had done well. He told me that it was important for me to understand my physical reality from as many perspectives as possible. As human beings we are often very limited in our perspective. Often our attention is so focused on making money or other material concerns, that we forget to enjoy life. Animals always reside in the moment. They never worry about the past, they enjoy life moment by moment. He said that we could learn a lot from animals, especially how our experience would change as we changed where we placed our attention. He told me that conserving energy was very important to a spiritual warrior. He warned me not to waste my energy trying to understand the unknowable.

I wanted to explore the concept of unknowable further, but Miguel was strangely silent. We walked slowly back to the cabin. The scene inside the cabin was mass chaos. Everyone was attempting to fix breakfast in a very small kitchen. I grabbed a banana and went out onto the back deck. Miguel was standing there, looking down at the valley.

Usually when he was like this I left him alone. I began to ask him about the chaos inside. I asked him why he fostered a sense of competition among the students. He told me that it was the way of power. I saw it as a residue of the old ones. When I mentioned that, he seemed very annoyed. There was no longer any gentleness in his look. For a moment I wondered what it would feel like to be a wart hog. I smiled nervously and Miguel turned around and continued looking at the valley. I went back inside.

A short time later Miguel came in and seated himself next to the fireplace. The students gathered around him, and he slowly began to speak. He warned us of the dangers of power. He said that it was very easy to lose our way if we weren't clear about our intentions. He said that some of the people in this room would misuse the power and use its dark side. He said he had been meditating on what to do about it. He said he wasn't sure if he should continue to teach those students. The way of power had always been well-guarded from those who had the potential to misuse it. He said he had concluded that the power itself was a great guardian. Warriors would only grow so far if they were not pure of heart and intention.

Power is an awesome gift as well as responsibility. It can be a loving teacher or a violent task master. The choice is ours. Did we want to waste this lifetime trying to understand the unknowable or did we want to bask in the love of the universe? Did we want our lives to serve our own selfish needs or the needs of the many?

Some of the students began to fidget around uncomfortably. The atmosphere in the room was very thick and disconcerting.

No one was even willing to make eye contact. I had often asked Miguel why he continued to teach some of the students. One student in particular was so angry that I found him frightening. I had refused to participate when he lead the group in a meditation. I thought it was Miguel's duty to protect the knowledge. Miguel felt that it was his duty to teach everyone who came to him.

I found myself gently closing my eyes and beginning to slip into a meditation. I saw everyone in the group as pure energy. At that level there was no competition or wrong intentions. We were all the same, pure love. I realized that some of my fellow students might lose their way for this lifetime, but eventually they would come back to the truth. There was nothing to fear and I returned with a sense of relief.

Miguel smiled as I opened my eyes and asked me to share what I had just seen. I did and a little bit later the group began to disperse. As we left the mountains later that day, I had a sense that this would be the last time I saw some of the people in the group. I was also aware that I no longer had any judgements about them, I was neutral at long last.

A few days later, as I was walking along the beach, I found myself face to face with a stranger who was dressed all in black. He looked sinister and I was immediately afraid. I anxiously looked around and found the beach was empty. I realized I had slipped into another reality without even realizing it. I was terrified and immediately started to run. As I ran headlong down the beach, I remembered one of the apprentices telling me not to be confused by appearances. Just because he was dressed in black did not mean he was evil, so I decided to trust my heart. As I started to feel him or sense his nature, I realized that he was gentle and not at all frightening. I slowed down and turned to face him.

He smiled and told me that I learned well. He told me that my heart would always guide me correctly if I listened to it and not to my mind. He said he was here to teach me about invisibility. He gently pulled his cloak around me and then he left. I found myself standing on the beach once again filled with other people. I walked along and said hello to some people I knew, but they ignored me. I was curious but continued on my way.

When I got up the next morning, I had forgotten about the stranger on the beach. I went to work and again noticed people were ignoring me. By lunchtime I was getting annoyed. Even when I went up to people and asked them questions they acted like I wasn't there. I began to get paranoid and wondered what I had done to everyone. When I got home from work, even my dog barely greeted me.

I went to the beach for my afternoon walk and I remembered the stranger. I was wondering how I could find him when I noticed I was alone on the beach. I figured he wouldn't be far off. As I continued to walk along, I felt his presence beside me long before I saw him. He smiled and asked me how I had enjoyed being invisible for the day. I noticed his smile and wondered if all teachers smile like that at their students. My next thought was relief which was quickly followed by anger. The dark stranger just continued to smile. He said that being invisible was a great gift. It was a tool I could use for protection, as well as to gain power. He told me that I could become invisible and observe others so I would know what their true intentions were, then I would know how to act. He said I could use it to sneak up on my opponents. I wasn't sure if I wanted to do that.

He told me invisibility was a gift he offered to few people. I asked him why he had come to me and he said because I had an open heart. Energetically he showed me how to cloak myself and become invisible. I had little difficulty becoming invisible, but I had a hard time becoming visible again. At times I still find that I hide behind that cloak and have to remind myself it is alright to step into the spotlight. He told me to explore my gift and to enjoy it. I once again found myself back on the beach filled with people. I hadn't realized how quiet his world was.

Exercise Nine

Developing your ability to feel the energy around us at all times merely takes practice. Find a park bench or some place you can sit undisturbed and observe people. I wear sunglasses so no one notices that I am watching. Close your eyes and feel people's energy. Pay attention to how your energy field distorts or changes as someone else walks into it. Get a feel for what is happening and then open your eyes. See if you were accurate. Can you tell the difference between children and adults? See what you "know" about them by just observing them.

This is a good exercise to help you go beyond your limited perceptions of the universe. Our minds filter out so much. Our perception of reality limits our experience of life. Without looking, try to remember what colors are present in the room in which you are sitting. Spend at least part of a day consciously noticing everything about your surroundings.

What do you filter out of your consciousness?

How often are you in touch with your intuition and what happens when you don't listen to it?

When you "know" something negative, do you act on it or ignore it?

How does it serve you to remain unaware of information about yourself?

◆◆◆◆◆◆◆◆◆◆◆ 10 ◎ ◆◆◆◆◆◆◆◆◆◆◆

STALKERS AND DREAMERS

*Only the dreamer
can change the dream.*

The classes were changing again. Miguel said it was important for the apprentices to teach as well as study. He assured us that the students pushed the teacher to learn faster. Sarita's first group of apprentices had taken three years to get to the same level that we reached in less than a year. Miguel said his learning had accelerated immensely since he began teaching us. He informed us that a new class would be starting in a few weeks and it would be the responsibility of several of us to teach the new students. This first class was a subject of a great deal of nervous speculation. Our nervousness was ironic because on the first night the students already viewed us as experts.

Francisco was in charge of the first class. He was a very humble soul who, like Miguel, was struggling to master the English language. He nervously began the class, pausing frequently to make sure he was using the proper words. He explained the nature of the universe in a halting fashion. Miguel finished the lecture, smiled and said, if you have any questions ask him, pointing towards Francisco. Francisco looked like he wanted to crawl under the rug. The rest of the class went smoothly.

My original class had continued to dwindle in size. There was now a mixture of apprentices along with a few curious students. As well as attending and teaching classes, many of the apprentices were studying privately with Miguel. A few days later all the apprentices gathered at the temple so that we could do a group meditation. I was in a very deep meditative state when I felt myself being attacked. I had been flying around in my eagle form, enjoying the sense of freedom I always received.

I was feeling totally relaxed, when suddenly I was attacked by another eagle. At first I was startled and wanted to fly away, but the other eagle continued to pursue me. I immediately began to fight back. I knew that if I lost a battle on this level I could be seriously injured or killed. The battle became quite pitched and I was loosing. Suddenly I changed animal forms and became a big cat. When the eagle swooped down at me again, I put my paw up with the claws out and impaled the bird. At that instant I found myself back in the room feeling very dazed.

I immediately went over to one of the more advanced apprentices and told her what had happened. She was very concerned and checked my ethereal body to see if I had been wounded. I hadn't been harmed, so she became even more concerned because she wanted to know who had attacked me. I felt guilty about hurting the other eagle, but she told me that I had acted properly. She told me to that from now on I must be vigilant during my meditations and make sure I protected myself at night.

When we told Miguel he said that he had been concerned that something like this would happen. Our group had been growing in power and was bound to attract the attention of other bands. He said that soon it would be time for us to become warriors and learn how to steal power. The thought made me uncomfortable. I had never understood the concept of competition to begin with, and being attacked for my power did not seem like fun. Stealing power and competition did not seem very spiritual to me. I did not want to believe that fighting was a necessary part of spirituality. When I asked Miguel, he said that being a warrior was part of the way of the Nagual. I just chalked it up to someone's misinterpretation of the information.

The idea of competition and fighting struck me as a very male interpretation of spiritual energy. I just "knew" they were unnecessary practices, but I was still too unsure of myself to confront Miguel with my feelings. Later, when Miguel told me that I was finished as his student, he also told me to go and teach in my own way. My way does not include competition or violence in any form. At that time I merely concentrated on learning how to access energy in the clearest possible way.

A long time ago Miguel had explained to me how people received and processed information from the ethereal levels. He said that there were two ways we could receive information: the way of the dreamer or the way of the stalker. He went on to say that people were usually predominately one or the other, although we could use both methods. They are very unique ways of accessing information and one is not inherently better then the other. In a sense it is like being right- or left-handed. Neither hand is inherently better than the other, but we are usually more comfortable using one more than the other.

Dreamers are people who have visions or see things in story form during their meditations. They see pictures and then they have to interpret the information. What happens energetically is that they receive ethereal energy or the information, then the energy triggers the brain's memory banks. The person then begins to see pictures. These pictures are interpreted according to the person's beliefs, individual symbolism, and desires. In a sense the information has to get translated twice, first by the mind, then by the person.

Stalkers are people that just know information. They have no idea where the information came from or how they know it, they are just certain that they know it. Stalkers don't need to translate the energy, it is presented to them in a finished form. Energetically they receive the information as a solid block of knowledge. When Miguel told me that I was a stalker, it cleared up a lot of the confusion I had been having. All my life I had "known" things and had no idea how I knew them. It also explained to me why I seldom saw visions in my meditations, but I usually came back with a lot of information.

Miguel said that each manner of receiving energy had its drawbacks. It is very easy for dreamers to get lost in their dreams and go crazy. They could also misinterpret their dreams and lose the true meaning of the energy. The stalker had to be vigilant and stay open to receiving the energy. Stalkers had to remain alert because the universe seldom sent advanced warnings about incoming messages.

During the next class Miguel began to talk about discipline. He said that it was time for all of us to become more disciplined. We had to be very dedicated at this point on our path. He reminded the class about the "old ones." The old ones had believed that they had to conquer death, and to do so they needed to accumulate a great deal of power. One of the easiest ways to gather that power was to steal it from other Naguals and their bands. Many of the Naguals in Mexico still lived by the these teachings. My attack was evidence that our group had been noticed. It was time, we had to learn how to defend ourselves.

Miguel said that an excellent way to become more vigilant and disciplined was to learn how to be lucid dreamers. In lucid dreaming the dreamer becomes aware of being asleep while they are still sleeping. Once the dreamer "wakes up" in the dream, they can begin to change the dream and control it. If you wake up in a dream and you are being chased, you could change your size, leave, or begin to chase the chaser. Miguel said that once we were awake in our dreams, we could travel, gather information, and increase our power. He said that it was also the first step towards being able to bi-locate, or be in two places at the same time.

Miguel went on to say that lucid dreaming was a very difficult skill to develop. We would really have to discipline ourselves. He said that if we put a great deal of our attention into learning how to be lucid while we were dreaming, we would succeed. The hardest part would be becoming aware while we were still in the dream. Miguel said that he used snoring as a mental alarm clock. While he was asleep, he would hear his snoring and that would remind him to wake up in his dreams.

He said that if we would concentrate on waking up in our dreams before we went to sleep, eventually we would succeed. Miguel also said we could look for a mirror while we were dreaming and look into it. He said that it would assist us in becoming aware in our dreams. There was something about the suggestion that made my skin crawl. I had a mental image of seeing something horrible in the mirror. He stressed again that we really had to have a strong desire in order to succeed and become lucid dreamers.

One of my first thoughts was that I would like to learn how to bi-locate so I could send the other me to work. My second thought was that, when I go to sleep at night, I didn't want to be "waking up" to work. I just wanted to sleep at night. I frequently looked forward to those periods of being unconscious. Since I had begun studying with Miguel, my dreams had become very strange anyway. I was not at all sure I wanted to wake up and actively participate in them. A long time ago Miguel had suggested that I start keeping a journal of all of my dreams. He now reminded us that a dream journal was one of the first steps towards lucid dreaming because it would teach us to remember our dreams.

The meditation that night was fairly uneventful. For a change when Miguel began to work in my power points I was able to relax, and I gently reminded myself that I was safe. When I came out of my meditation, I remembered that Miguel and Sarita had been frequent visitors in my dreams lately. As the class began to disperse, several of us lingered outside the temple and began to compare notes about our dreams. Each of us remembered having similar experiences in which Sarita and Miguel came to get us at night. Miguel had that smile on his face as he walked past us towards his car.

As I drove home from class that night, I began to think about lucid dreaming. I began to compare my life to a dream. For many years I had been asleep, I had thought life was very real and concrete. I had totally accepted all the beliefs and truths society and my parents had taught me. When I had begun my studies, I had actually started to wake up. I began to question my beliefs and my experiences. In a sense I was beginning to change the contents of my life, or the dream I had been living. I realized that I could view my awakening as a process of becoming lucid in my own life. I could wake up and begin to change my life. Life could really be a process during which we learn about lucid living.

A few nights later I had an incredibly vivid dream. I found myself flying along in my human form doing loops and just having a great time. I was flying very rapidly over some power lines when I spotted one of the other apprentices standing on the ground below me. I swooped down and hovered above her. We began talking and she told me I couldn't do that. At first I was concerned. Then I looked at her and said I was flying, so obviously I could. I asked her if she would like to join me. She hesitated for a minute, then we took off together. After a short time we began to race with one another. We were having a wonderful time. We flew past two men working on telephone poles and scared the daylights out of them. We both laughed, then I woke up.

When I got up the next morning, I was very excited about the dream, and I was still amused by the look on the two men's faces. Later that day I saw my friend, and before I had a chance to say anything she asked me if I had dreamt about flying. I said I had and we compared notes, the only real difference was she didn't remember scaring the two men.

Each morning I wrote down all my dreams. I seemed to be remembering more of them every day, and they continued to be intense. I found myself spending a great deal of time with Miguel and Sarita. In one particularly vivid dream, I remember them talking very rapidly in Spanish. I was feeling left out when I said to myself, this is a dream, if I want to I can understand Spanish. At that instant I could understand everything they were saying. At the time I didn't realize I was actually lucid dreaming.

Sarita immediately began to talk to me about the power of our feminine nature. She said that Naguals always had women in their bands because of their power. In fact women were much more powerful beings than men. Feminine energy was directly linked to one's spiritual essence. She told me that it was easy to lose sight of why we were studying and to forget the importance of our connection with our femininity. After all, the only real power is spiritual, everything else is an illusion.

Society has always emphasized the value of male energy. In most communities, women were thought of as second class citizens. Sarita said it had been a real struggle for her during her studies because of those limiting beliefs. In her generation, female children were still frequently killed at birth. They certainly weren't valued. She said one of her most difficult challenges was to overcome her negative programming—the belief that men were of greater value then women. Until she overcame that programming, she was unable to become the powerful healer and teacher she was now. She said many men challenged her right to be powerful and tried to steal her power. Eventually she had triumphed and now she was greatly respected, even revered.

Sarita pointed out that if we looked at history, most of the great teachers had been men. In the past, the time had not been right to break those traditions, now it was. It is time for us to reclaim and revere the feminine. The feminine is one with Mother Earth. Only women and gods are able to create life. Humans have come forth from the womb of Mother Earth so we could remember the truth. We were born so we could remember we are one with the great Creator. Our happiness results from surrendering our will to the Creator and returning home. We have always been one with that great creative energy. We have never really left home in the first place, we just think we have. Reclaiming the female part of ourselves and accepting the power and beauty of it is the first step in being able to go home again.

Sarita said she was saddened because it is mainly women who teach other women to hate their femininity. We must embrace our femininity. We have to reclaim our softness and remember that our strength comes from that vulnerability. We can never be safe hiding behind walls of protection or behind men. We will only be safe when we have reclaimed our birthright, our own feminine power. For too long we have endeavored to strengthen the male part of ourselves. The male energy is already finely tuned, it is time to do the same for our feminine side.

She reminded me that this message was for men as well as women. It is a time for all of us to live with a greater sense of balance and harmony. The time for fighting and competition is over. It is time to realize that true power and strength can only be found in the power of love and acceptance. She told me to study the attributes of women. I would find true strength in the ways of the female. Females had always been the lovers, the compassionate ones. Women had always known how to nurture the family. She told me to embrace that strength and wisdom now. She said that only women could be powerful in their own right and that males needed the female energy to be complete.

When I awoke in the morning, I was amazed. Sarita had always talked to me and welcomed me warmly whenever she saw me, but I had never understood what she was saying. I stayed in bed for quite awhile musing about what she had said. It was a vast contrast to the way society viewed male and female roles.

A few days later I told Miguel about my dream. He was excited, but he also seemed a bit annoyed or embarrassed. Later on, when I mentioned Miguel's reaction to one of the female apprentices, she laughed. She said Sarita often teased Miguel about his beliefs on male superiority. It was an interesting time of exploration as I began to step more fully into my feminine center.

Each day I began to feel more whole and complete. Judgements I had carried for years began to change into compassion. I felt softer and at the same time stronger. I noticed I had begun to carry my body differently. I felt a sense of peace much of the time. Each time Sarita saw me she would smile broadly and nod her head in approval. I certainly hadn't expected this when I began concentrating on learning to become a lucid dreamer.

EXERCISE TEN

In order to learn how to be a lucid dreamer, you must first learn how to remember your dreams. Before going to sleep at night, remind yourself to remember your dreams. Keep a pad and pen at your bedside and as soon as you wake up, write down your dreams. If you have a hard time remembering them, drink several glasses of water before bedtime. When you get up during the night to go to the bathroom you will remember your dreams.

Once you can remember all of your dreams, you can begin to practice lucid dreaming. When you go to bed at night, remind yourself to wake up in your dreams while remaining asleep. Keep doing this nightly until you do. It takes some people years to do this, while others are able to do it immediately.

Dreams are also a gateway to your psyche. You can use your dream journal to gain insight into yourself. The meanings of some dreams are self-evident, while others are more subtle. You can always view your dreams from many different perspectives and levels. Each person has their own internal symbolism, so dream books are not that useful. You may have different meanings than the author for your symbols. Take one of your dreams and ask yourself the following questions.

First look at the surface meaning. What does the story tell you? What message does this dream have for me?

Are the players in the dream familiar, who do they represent? What are they trying to tell you?

Next allow yourself to become each person and element in the dream and ask yourself the following questions.

What message do you have for me and what do you represent to me?

How can you help me? Why have you come to me?

How can I use this information to transform my life?

When you feel you understand the dream, thank it for coming. If you are still unsure of the meaning, ask to have another dream the next night to help you understand this dream. You can also use your dreams to gather specific information. After you are able to remember your dreams, ask to have a dream about a specific subject that you will remember and understand.

MAGIC AND POWER

Imagine the best possible thing that could happen in your life and know that the universe can imagine it even better.

After the dream I had with Sarita, my life took on a surreal quality. I had always been somewhat of a tomboy, so getting in touch with my feminine side was wonderful. I was terrified at times with my vulnerability, but it did feel good to be soft and gentle. The more vulnerable I was, the more my life seemed to be filled with magical events.

One day as I was walking along the beach with my dog, some people stopped me. They pointed towards a group of fish right off shore and asked me what they were. I looked, and to my amazement saw dolphins. I had never seen dolphins there before, nor had I ever seen them that close to shore. I could feel their presence within my psyche, they were gentle and loving. They began to talk to me about creation. I could not quite understand what they were saying, but the experience was magical.

When I told Miguel about the experience he smiled and said creation was really a form of magic. He told me he was going to teach us a class on magic. When he said that, I had a mental image of him showing up in a cape and pulling rabbits out of a hat. Instead he began by drawing the following diagram:

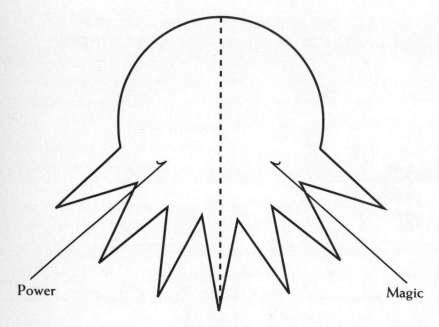

Power   Magic

FIGURE 11-1

This diagram represents the universe in its entirety. Miguel drew a line down the center of the diagram and labeled one side power and the other side magic. He said they were mirror images of one another. Magic was power that had been transformed into physical form. Power was potential energy, or energy that was waiting to be used. Every day we used magic, usually unconsciously. Our bodies are great magicians, they constantly transform food into energy and energy into action.

In order to understand magic, Miguel said that we needed to understand how we really create our reality. He told us that magic was merely our ability to transform energy into physical form. We constantly do that on a daily basis. Our task as spiritual seekers was to begin manipulating this energy consciously. The great masters were able to perform feats that seemed like miracles because they understood the laws of the physical universe and were able to use them to their advantage.

The first step in understanding those laws is understanding the self. The energy must flow through our minds first. So if our minds are cluttered with conflicting thoughts and beliefs, the energy is diffused or distorted. We must see ourselves clearly and know what we want and why we want it before we can begin to successfully create it. The energy of creation follows our attention, our thoughts, and our emotions.

Physical manifestation always follows an idea, a thought, or emotion. It is almost as though each of them helps the energy to condense, then something manifests. We all have the ability to create at all levels of our consciousness. Frequently we are unaware of the level we are creating from. Often we create the very things we fear the most because the emotion of fear is so intense. The more powerfully we feel about something, the more rapidly we manifest it. This is also true of our intentions and attention. The more focused we are, the quicker things manifest.

Most of our reality is controlled by our beliefs. Whatever we believe we manifest. Our minds are very much like computers that are programmed to continuously prove our beliefs by creat-

ing circumstances to reaffirm them. As adults we seldom question our beliefs, we just manifest our lives so those beliefs seem
true. Miguel suggested that if we wanted to change the results
we were getting in our lives, we should check our beliefs.

For instance someone can have a strong belief in karma
which explains karma as a system of cause and effect in which
errors are automatically punished. If that person hurt someone,
even if it was unintentional, they would believe they were going
to get punished. At some level, they would allow something to
happen so it appeared as if they had been punished. If the same
event happened and the belief was not present the punishment
would not occur.

One of the students said that he thought karma was a universal law so it would work regardless of whether the person
believed in it or not. Miguel said karma was a universal law but
not as it was traditionally defined. Karma is merely another way
to explain that human beings need to learn lessons. It is not punishment. The whole purpose of our existence is to remember
that we are one with the Creator. In a sense our karma is any
belief that stops us from experiencing that oneness. Karma is
really about changing our beliefs and perception of the world.
So it does work automatically, but not as a form of judgement. It
helps remind us where the magic really exists.

Magic happens every time we change the way we look at
things or the way in which we experience life. As soon as we
change our perspective, our reality changes. If we believe in
tests and punishment, chances are that our life has been difficult.
If we change our perspective and begin to believe in growth and
the process of learning, life becomes easier and more enjoyable.

Magic is constantly happening in our life, power is always changing into physical reality. All we really need is the courage to squarely face our past and change our perspective about it. We need to become self-aware. We must become conscious of our decisions. We have to realize that most of them are made based on facts that other people have told us about ourselves and the world. Most of our beliefs are based on information we received as a child. Many of us continue to make decisions based on information that was inaccurate at best thirty years ago, and today it is totally useless. We continue to stay in the security point that was created for us as a child. It is time to separate our emotions from our actions and start making decisions based on the present rather than the past. The only time magic can happen is in the present or in the moment we call now.

When Miguel asked if there were any questions, everyone looked pretty confused or overwhelmed. I had expected specific steps. I hoped he was going to say, "Ok now, if you do x, y, and z, you will always create whatever it is that you want." I later realized that in a sense he had. Miguel had told us to become aware of our beliefs and change them if we wanted different results.

We took a short break and then we got ready for a meditation. Miguel placed me in the center of the triangle. It had been a long time since I meditated there. I was excited because I usually had intense experiences while seated there.

The lights were dimmed and I could feel Miguel working in my power points. I settled back and a few moments later I could feel my consciousness leaving my body. I found myself traveling through space. Way out in the darkness I saw what appeared to be a mountaintop. As I stood on the mountaintop, I could see time spread out below me. I instinctively knew that I was standing at the point where time and infinity intersect. I realized that the point of intersection was the moment we call now. In that instant I knew that time was an illusion, it was a construct of our minds. Time was an attempt to put order into a universe our minds could not understand.

As I stood there eternity was spread out below me. It was a magnificent tapestry of energy and lights. Words could never do it justice. I felt so many of my beliefs crumbling. Reality was not at all how I had perceived it. Reality as I knew it was an illusion, and the illusion was controlled by my beliefs. Whatever I believed, I saw in front of me in three-dimensional, living color.

I was overwhelmed. I stood there and silently wept at the beauty and the freedom I saw. As I continued to view the scene, I began to understand so much. I realized if I changed my beliefs, I could change my world. My experience of life really did reside between my ears. I was free to choose new beliefs and experiences at any point in time. Things I never even realized I was confused about suddenly became clear. It took me years to fully assimilate the experience.

The scene was composed of interlinking filaments of light. They looked like luminescent fibers that were woven into an intricate web of patterns. The patterns they produced were magnificent. Slowly I began to see order in the patterns. There was a definite flow and harmony to the tapestry.

As I began to look at the scene more closely, I noticed that along the filaments there were places where there was a greater energy concentration. These points looked like round orbs of intense light. From each of these points, a large number of new filaments originated. After a time I knew that each of these points was a place where a decision of some sort had been made. Each filament looked like a lifeline and from each decision a number of a new lifetimes originated. Some of the lifelines seemed brighter than others. Some ended rather abruptly. Some of the lines lead back to the source, others went on to other dimensions or new lifetimes.

I began to see how life had a flow or a sense of harmony to it. Our choices and decisions were not really random, there was a definite pattern. At first the mosaic looked like a maze, but as I pulled on the individual strands everything made sense. I also began to realize that the mosaic had another dimension. By exerting pressure on it, the tapestry would bend much like a trampoline. When that happened, energy would seemingly flow into the depression to fill it.

As I moved closer to the tapestry, I became caught up in the fibers. Almost at once I lost my perspective, and I forgot that I was merely on a filament of time. That filament became very real and I rapidly became a part of it. I began to live that life. As I began to separate and regain my perspective, I could see where each choice would lead me. Some of the strands felt familiar, but I knew that they didn't lead home. Choosing the familiar strands would merely cause more of the same old experiences. Other strands felt challenging, but I knew they would lead me closer to my spiritual center. I could choose whichever one I wanted.

Eventually I found myself again standing on the mountaintop in awe. The universe was incredibly beautiful from this perspective. It was filled with sparkles and was so bright. It reminded me of the Milky Way on a clear, moonless night. Perhaps that was why I had always been so fascinated by the stars. I heard Miguel's voice off in the distance. I did not want to return to the temple.

As we went around the room and shared our experiences I tried putting words to mine. I found it very difficult to convey the sense of freedom and the knowledge about the power of choice I had received on that mountain top. Everything Miguel had ever said about intentions, where we placed our attention, separating our emotions from our actions, and all the other countless lessons, suddenly made sense. Each of those lessons was about leaving the mind behind and moving into that spiritual center. Years later I realized that my mind could not go to that mountaintop with me, it was strictly in the realm of spirit. When I tried to express those feelings, Miguel just smiled knowingly at me.

At the end of class that night Miguel announced that it was time for our Fire Initiation. I was excited and nervous. When Miguel was asked how to prepare for this initiation, he responded with his usual "however you want to prepare." He told each of us to bring a white candle. He had been talking privately to me about this initiation for some time. Miguel told me that the Fire Initiation was much more intense than the Water Initiation. It would be a time when we would be tested and only those that could withstand the power of the flame would survive. Fire had been used for years as a purifying agent and swords were tempered in the flame to give them strength.

As the time for the Fire Initiation had drawn closer, many of the students had indeed dropped out of the class. Most of them had decided that there was something wrong with Miguel or with one of the other students. Very few of the original people I began studying with were left in the group. Many people had come and gone, but very few had been willing to walk through the upheaval this path seemed to cause in their personal lives. After my meditation, I realized that the turmoil really came from our persistence in trying to go back to the familiar. This path did not allow for that option. It constantly expanded the security point into unknown regions. My mind definitely had a hard time with a lot of the information I had received while I had been studying with Miguel.

I drove home lost in thought. I knew that I was about to enter a new dimension. A large part of me just wanted life to be "normal" again. I was tired of changes. I was tired of becoming birds and cats and standing on mountaintops.

After I got done having my mental temper tantrum, I smiled. I was very grateful for the perspective that meditation had given me that night. I only hoped that I would retain that vision. I knew only too well from past experiences that the insight would go and I would have to remember it all over again. The path home to my spiritual center definitely seemed to be one of two steps forward, then one backwards. At least I was at the stage that I remembered that it was a process. As I exited the freeway and saw the lights below me, I was amazed at how far I had come. I said a little prayer of thanks that I had persevered.

EXERCISE ELEVEN

Magic always occurs in my life as soon as I become able or willing to change my perspective. Changing my perspective is merely a matter of looking at my world in a different manner. One of the best ways I know of to do that is by playing with nature. When I go out in nature and really experience the peaceful energy of trees, rocks, and water I get out of myself.

The wind had always been my ally. Frequently the wind will remind me to get out of myself when I am very upset. One night I was sitting outside obsessing about something and the wind came up. As it swirled around me I remembered I had a choice, I could remain miserable or change my thinking. That night I chose to change my thinking. Experiment with the wind. Notice it, really feel it, and let it help you get out of your mind.

Trees also contain magical energy. Find a tree where you won't be disturbed and lean against it. Call upon the elements of earth, wind, water, and fire. Ask them in the form of a simple prayer to help cleanse and guide you. Ask the tree to assist you. Close your eyes and open yourself up, allow yourself to feel the presence of the tree. As you feel its energy running through you, your body will begin to gently rock. When the tree is done the rocking will stop. Thank the tree for its energy and its presence in your life.

Begin to experience nature as being truly alive. Sit by a rock and allow it to talk to you. Go in the water and open up and allow yourself to feel its love surround you. Listen to the wind talk to you. All of these exercises take patience, an open mind, and practice. Give yourself a gift by taking time to become aware of the magic nature has to offer. Take time to list all the magical things that have already happened in your life.

Just think of the mathematical probability of you sitting where you are at this moment in time reading this book. Think of the number of events that it took to bring you to this point in time. The numbers are astronomical. Your parents had to be born, they had to come together, and… Allow yourself to acknowledge what a miracle you really are.

How do you define magic?

What do you think about miracles?

Do you deserve to have a magical life?

What could stop magic from happening in your life?

When something wonderful happens to a friend or acquaintance, how do you feel?

Make a decision to allow magic to begin working for you in your life.

12

THE FIRE INITIATION

There is a quiet still voice within each of us.
It has all of our answers if we are willing to listen.

As the day grew closer I found myself questioning whether I wanted to take the next step. After the Water Initiation, my life had become totally chaotic. Miguel told me this initiation was even more intense, and I was not sure if I was ready for any more earth-shattering life changes. I thought of the vision I had in my last meditation with the group and all my doubts left me. This was my path and, although I often went kicking and screaming, I knew I would always go where my heart led me.

This initiation was to take place at Miguel's home. He shared the house with Sarita and several of the original apprentices. The house sat on the side of a cliff overlooking the city. Off in the distance you could see the ocean. Although the house was in the middle of the city, it felt very private and secluded. The sky always seemed vast, and the view was expansive.

As I approached his street that night, my stomach did a slow roll and then tied itself into a knot. I tried telling myself I should be used to this sort of thing by now, but I wasn't. My mind wanted to be anywhere but here. As I walked through the house into the yard, I noticed the kitchen table was already full of plates overflowing with food. The house had a festive air, but as soon as I stepped out of the house into the yard the mood changed.

The yard was terraced and after the last terrace the cliff fell off sharply. As I looked at the yard, it seemed to be suspended in space. There was a large bonfire burning in the middle of it. Against the fence, at the far end of the yard, stood several of the apprentices. They all looked nervous and out of place. Miguel stood off to the side. He usually dressed in black, but tonight he was dressed all in white. He was strangely unapproachable.

Opposite the fence was a semicircle of chairs. Sister Sarita sat in the center. Her husband, a great healer in his own right, sat beside her. Around them stood the rest of their band. I had never met most of these people before, but I knew they were all power-ful beings. They formed a human altar. Behind them stood some of Sarita's older apprentices. The energy was almost overwhelm-ing as I took my place with the other apprentices. Everyone was silent and the whole place felt sacred. Usually when I was nervous I would joke around and make wisecracks, but tonight I felt very subdued. I knew this was a sacred and holy occasion.

Sarita raised her arms and the ceremony began. As she began to invoke the energies, the fire seemed to intensify and the logs began to snap. Sparks danced upwards into the night sky as if to answer her prayers. She placed a red poncho over Miguel's head. He slowly circled the fire, obviously in a deep trance. When he

stood in front of the altar again, he slowly took off the red poncho. The poncho had represented his physical form. He stood
there as the spiritual being he truly was. Then Miguel took the
power stick from Sarita and drew a circle around the bonfire.

He invoked the power of the four directions, then called
upon the beings of light to assist in this ceremony. He carefully
placed more advanced apprentices at each of the four corners.
Then Sarita stood up. She was also in a very deep trance. She
began a long prayer of invocation. She talked about the history
of this tradition. Originally the wisdom had been passed down
generation to generation, but now it was time for the knowledge
to become more widespread so this humanity could be saved.
Four humanities had come before us. Each one had gotten lost
and destroyed itself. Sarita said we had already gone beyond the
point in time where the humanities usually destroyed themselves. She said we had to remember our spiritual nature and go
home to the Father, or we too would destroy ourselves.

Sarita said that it was a time for balance and harmony. The
way of the old ones was the path of pain. The new path was one
of love and acceptance. She asked if we were willing to dedicate
ourselves to this quest. Most of us nodded in the affirmative.
The wind began to pick up and it became harder to hear the
interpreter. Sarita talked for quite a while longer, and then she
began to wobble and she sat down. Miguel made sure she was
comfortable, then he again picked up the power stick. I felt
myself going into an altered state. The roar of the fire was
beginning to make my head pound.

The next thing I knew, it was my turn to enter the circle. I
placed my candle in front of the fire and turned to face Miguel.

His eyes were like dark orbs. He handed me the power stick and told me to face the altar. I lifted the staff up over my head and took a deep breath. I knew it was my turn to call upon the power and tell the universe what my intentions were. I stood there nervously trying to decide what to say. I took another deep breath and using my best power voice I called upon the angels of light. I asked to be used as a channel for their healing energy. I asked for courage and wisdom. I asked that I always be guided in love towards the light. I told the universe I was willing to be used in any way to assist myself and others in going home. I felt a surge of power flowing through me. I felt incredibly small and humble, yet filled with power.

I turned and faced Miguel. He motioned towards my candle and indicated that it was time for me to bring it to him. He reached into the fire and pulled out a burning stick. He lit my candle and said that it symbolized the ethereal flame that burned within me. He asked the universe to assist my flame in burning ever brighter, and he asked for assistance and guidance for me. He told the universe that I was a great healer and teacher. He asked that I be provided with all the resources necessary for me to carry my message to those that needed it. He asked for the universe to bless my path.

I turned and again faced Sarita. She stood and she began to speak slowly in Spanish. I could barely hear the woman who was translating, but Sarita blessed me and talked about the many things I was meant to do. She reminded the universe and those present that I was a powerful woman blessed with many gifts from the Creator. She told me to use those gifts wisely and not to hide them behind false humility. The time would come when I would fully understand what I had been taught. I would truly be a woman of power and great wisdom. She again sat down.

I handed the power stick back to Miguel. As I walked out of the circle, I noticed that the horizon still had a faint pink after-glow from the sunset. I set my candle down in front of me and looked up at the sky. As I looked up there were millions of stars twinkling at me. My eyes filled with tears as I felt the love and the support of the universe gently enfold me. In that instant I felt totally supported and loved for the first time in my life. I had certainly come a long way from that scared little girl in New York who was afraid of infinity.

As the last apprentice moved out of the circle, Miguel began to erase it. He slowly thanked the spirits for their assistance and guidance. When he was done, he turned to Sarita. She motioned for several of the older apprentices to come forward. She did a consecration for them, much like the one she had done at the Water Initiation. I felt honored and privileged to witness this ancient and sacred ceremony.

When that ceremony was through, everyone linked hands and formed a huge circle around the bonfire. The fire had burned down, but it was still very bright. As I looked around the circle, people's eyes looked like mirrors reflecting the flames. Everyone looked peaceful and energized. The wind began to pick up and the night air had a definite chill to it. Sarita gave a final blessing and closed the ceremony. The group slowly began to disband. By the time we reached the house, I noticed that many of the people that had sat at the altar had disappeared, I don't know why that surprised me.

As I walked over to Miguel, music began to drift out of the house. I went over and gave him a hug. I tried to thank him, but he thanked me instead. He smiled and walked away. I made my way into the house. Everyone was in a very festive mood. There was a great deal of laughter and happiness. I was aware of what a vast contrast it was to my childhood. The adults in my world had always been very serious and usually angry. I sat down and watched the festivities. I noticed I was having a difficult time participating. I was unable to feel like I was a part of the group.

As I left Miguel's house that night, I felt strangely alone and melancholy. At first I decided that I felt that way because I was drained. After all, I reasoned, it had been a big day. I was tired and I had to go to work the next day. I got up the next morning and felt even worse. I vaguely remembered feeling this way after the Water Initiation, so I tried to trust the process. But the feelings still intensified. Once again all the unresolved issues and emotions from my past were coming up to the surface. I was not sure what to do with those memories and emotions.

During my morning meditation, I was reminded that the only time I ever experienced any pain was when I resisted change. I wondered how many more times I would need to be reminded of that. I realized that it was clearly time for me to make some dramatic shifts in the way I lead my life, but I wasn't willing to make those changes yet. It didn't take very long before I was in enough emotional pain that I decided to let go. I eventually changed jobs and decided to move. A few nights later I began to get answers to my questions about how to release the past.

Shortly after the initiation I began to have a series of intense dreams. For a period of about two weeks, each morning when I awoke I felt as if I had never really slept. My memory of the dreams was hazy, but I knew they were important. After a few days I felt like a walking zombie because I was so tired. I walked around each day in a fog. One morning the dreams stopped. While I was standing next to the phone the following day, I heard a voice tell me to write the dreams down. The voice was so vivid that I looked around to see who was speaking. I decided, that in a few days when I was more rested, I would write them down. I tried to go about my day, but I was so haunted by the dreams that I finally began to write them down.

While I had been dreaming, the dreams had been hazy. I was totally unclear about what was going on. As I began to write, I realized that I had been dreaming about a series of exercises and meditations that would assist people in clearing out the emotions from their past. One night I would dream about the information, and on the following night I would dream about the exercises. By the time I was finished writing, I had all the material necessary for a series of six classes. I was amazed and very excited. I was also afraid that I was losing touch with reality. Receiving information for a class at night was not part of my "normal" process.

As I began to work through the exercises myself, much of my emotional turmoil began to dissipate. I contacted several friends and shared the information with them. They thought that the class outline was wonderful. I talked to the owners of a local New Age bookstore, and they asked me if I wanted to teach classes there. Eventually as I understood the information myself and experienced its effectiveness, I taught a six-week class based on the information. The class was very well received.

The class revolved around the concept that each one of us is one hundred percent responsible for everything we experience in our lives. As children we had been "victims" of our parents beliefs and emotions. As adults we need to begin to sort out the information we have received and develop our own definitions. The way we experience the events in our life depends on those definitions. After all no one really has the power to upset us. We upset ourselves by what we tell ourselves about what happens. Our actions are usually controlled by what we tell ourselves. As I began to think about the power we have as individuals to change our lives by changing our thoughts, I realized how much freedom we abdicate when we find it necessary to be right. As I have stated previously, I found that very early in my studies I noticed that my mind would rather be right than happy.

So often I had allowed myself to be victimized by my thoughts and my emotions. I began to see just how important it was to separate my emotions from my actions. As long as they were tied together in any way, I was doomed to repeat the past. My emotions would cause me to make the same choices over and over again. Naturally the same choices would lead to a rerun of the past.

The class also stressed acceptance. I saw clearly how judgement of any sort limited my possibilities. I realized that as soon as I judged anything or anyone, I was immediately in a defensive position or a position of weakness. I saw how clearly any judgement came from a belief in my own unworthiness. I was surprised that forgiveness was also included in the category of judgement. Slowly I began to realize that in order for me to forgive someone or something, I had to stand in judgment of the

Do you feel you need to lose weight or change something about your-self in order to be happy?

Do you want a better relationship, a better job, or more money?

Do you want to be more spiritual or wiser?

What are you waiting for, what do you need to be happy?

Your mind has an endless list of unfulfilled desires. It usually adds things to the list much faster then we can acquire them. Notice how that type of thinking keeps you out of the moment. If you wait until tomorrow for your happiness, you will wait for-ever—like the song says, tomorrow is always a day away.

How do you judge yourself and others?

How do you define yourself?

Where does your self-worth and happiness come from?

Remember it is all an inside job. There is no out there, out there is only a reflection of what is going on inside of each of us.

13

PERSONAL POWER & PERSONAL IMPORTANCE

Fear lives in our mind,
peace comes from our heart.

In the course of my studies, I saw many people get lost in their egos. Inevitably they would begin to use their power for selfish or nonproductive reasons. They would eventually turn to the "dark side of the force." I remember sitting in a movie theater watching *Return of the Jedi*. In the movie Luke finds out who his father really is and that he used to be a Jedi knight. Luke feels totally betrayed and confused by the seeming conflict between evil and good. As my studies continued I realized that Darth Vader had merely gotten caught up in his ego. Spiritual energy was never meant to be controlled by our egos or our minds.

The force, God, or whatever we choose to call that energy is really all there is. At the spiritual level there is no duality, there is no separation between ourselves, each other, and the life force. Good and evil are constructs of our minds and egos. On the physical level, good and evil certainly appear to exist separately, but they are actually one.

Good and evil are really two sides of the same coin. If we split a coin down the center, where does the head's side end and the tail's side start? No matter how thinly we slice a coin, there is always a head's side and a tail's side. As long as we remain in the realm of ego or the physical universe, we will have this sense of duality. There will always be right and wrong, good and evil, birth and death. Once we step beyond that sense of duality, we step into the realm of spirit or the realm of miracles.

One afternoon Miguel and I were discussing personal power. He used one of the other students as an example. This particular student had a huge ego. He was always telling people what a wonderful healer he was and how powerful he was. From my perspective, his life was a mess. He had very little integrity and he frequently harmed other people with his actions. Miguel suggested that his power was actually personal importance rather than power. He went on to say that personal importance is one of the greatest traps of the spiritual warrior. If we have a great deal of ego, or personal importance, we actually cut ourselves off from our connection with our spiritual center. The only true power comes from that spiritual center, all else is an illusion. When people work from the level of ego, they are working in illusions. Con artists are masters at that sort of illusion. They feed a person's ego and are able to manipulate people into doing whatever it is that they want them to do.

Spiritual people never have to "sell" their ideas. They just seem to have a sense of serenity, sincerity, and honesty that lets most people know that they are telling the truth. For me the truth seems to resonate in my body. Whenever I deal with the truth, I have a sense of ease and comfort. I feel relaxed and at peace. I never feel confused or tense, unless I am trying to convince myself of something that is not true. Whenever I deal with ego-based theories disguised as truths, I feel out of balance or ill at ease. When confronted with someone who is working on the level of pure ego or when my ego is in the way, I often feel crazy.

Dealing with ego based "truths" reminds me of my childhood. Frequently there would be an elephant (some huge issue) in the living room, and the rest of the family would pretend it wasn't there. When I would say look at the elephant, everyone would tell me that I was crazy. The ego will often confuse us so we can't hear or see the truth. The ego always leaves us feeling unsatisfied and often confused.

Miguel explained that personal importance and personal power were inversely proportionate. If someone has a great deal of personal importance, they have very little personal power. Someone who has a great deal of personal power is humble, hence they have very little personal importance or ego. Personal power is something the spiritual warrior must always guard. Expanding one's power takes a lot of effort and dedication. That power is easily lost if a person starts believing he or she is the power, rather then merely a channel for it. The most beneficial attitude to have is one of humility, where your true intention is service to others. As soon as we become self-serving, we are cut off from our spiritual center and our power begins to fade.

As Miguel explained these concepts, I felt a tinge of fear and confusion. As I explored my fear, I realized that for the moment

I had slipped back into my old concept of God as a punishing being, one that keeps score. That old concept was so far from the truth I had to laugh. I realized that, in essence, Miguel was simply telling me to check my motives. I knew that my ego was a very slippery being. I could easily rationalize almost any decision I wanted to make if I listened to my ego. One more time I realized that the process really boiled down to listening to my heart and not my head.

Miguel frequently stressed the importance of conserving energy. He would laugh when I would endlessly ask him questions. He often told me that I loved to worry almost as much as I loved to live. I knew that my confusion about gaining personal power was another thing for me to worry about. My mind always told me that I wasn't doing things right. I reminded myself that I was indeed a powerful woman, and I had nothing to fear. Of course my next thought was that even thinking such a thought showed I was ego based. So I just told my mind to shut up.

My mind and I continued to have an extended conversation, when I noticed Miguel smiling at me. He asked me if I was done, or if I wanted to continue the debate for a while. I was always amazed when he seemed to read my mind like that. I smiled sheepishly and we continued talking for a while. He told me that next week he wanted me to teach class. I asked him about what and he just smiled.

The following week I knew it was time for me to take some sort of a leap, but I was terrified. Every time I meditated I could feel a sense of urgency, a call to do something. I was not really sure what it was, but I sensed that part of me didn't want to do it. I was terrified of doing it alone. So one day in my meditation

I told my guides that I would be willing to do whatever it was, but only if Miguel were present. The urgency stopped. I also knew that I had to follow through with this bargain.

As soon as Miguel arrived at the temple I told him about my sense of urgency. He smiled and told me he was glad that I was finally ready. The format of the class had been changed, we meditated first, then the lecture portion of the class followed. When most of the students had arrived Miguel began to set up the meditation. He had us sit in a star configuration. He and two other people sat back to back in a triangle. He had each person in the center pair off with someone so we could do a flying meditation. The person in the center would act as a ground, allowing the other person's emotions to flow through them effortlessly.

Miguel motioned for me to lie down in front of him. There were six of us in the center and the formation looked like a large starfish. It was a very powerful arrangement. The rest of the group sat around us in a circle. As soon as I lay down, I could feel the energy begin to surge through me. My heart began to pound, and I broke out in a cold sweat. I slowed my breathing and began to relax. I could feel Miguel working on my power points. Slowly my consciousness began to rise up out of my body.

At some level I was still aware of being terrified. As I drifted up out of my body, I began to recall a past life. I had been a student or initiate of a great teacher. In ancient times students would often be brought to the edge of death. They would often be given strong poisons and hallucinogens so their consciousness would leave their bodies. When they left the body, their consciousness would scatter throughout the universe and bring back knowledge. If the student died, his or her consciousness would be left drifting in millions of pieces. In that lifetime I had died. It had taken me what seemed like an eternity to reassemble myself. I now knew why I was so afraid. It was time for me to try the process again.

I found myself standing near the edge of a cliff. The sky had a surreal flat quality and was a pinkish-gray hue. I stood there nervously. I found myself running towards the edge of the cliff. Suddenly I felt like I had exploded. Part of me stood on the edge of the cliff while I watched the most amazing fireworks display I have ever seen. Then I realized that those little sparks of light were all me. I saw and felt millions of events that were all happening simultaneously. I saw time flying by at a tremendously rapid rate. Then I stood beyond time.

I saw the physical universe spread out below me. I seemed to be nowhere and everywhere all at once. Time and space seemed to have no meaning. Everything and everywhere was all right here and right now. I felt very powerful, at the same instant I felt very weak. I seemed to be caught in duality. If I felt large, I also felt small. I began to realize that everything was merely one side of a coin or the other. There was no black or white, there was black-white. My perspective continuously shifted and changed. I was unable to judge anything because everything kept shifting.

Suddenly I found myself viewing the creation of the physical universe. I stood there in wonder and awe. First there was an immense being of light. It was infinite. It always had been and always would be. There was no beginning or end. I felt like I was standing inside a huge womb of pure unconditional love. I was one with that energy and there was absolutely no sense of separation. I had never felt so totally loved and nurtured.

Then everything began to shift and change. The whole scene began to bubble and churn. It looked like someone had opened a warm bottle of beer, and foam was spreading out all over. One moment I was one with everything and in the next moment I was aware of myself as a separate entity. I felt incredibly alone. Instead of viewing the whole scene, I was now one of those tiny bubbles, totally unaware of any other bubbles. The loneliness was compounded by the sense of oneness I had felt the moment before.

A few moments later I was again viewing the scene from above. I was aware of the intense loneliness of some of the individual beings. Some of the beings seemed to maintain their sense of connection, while others felt totally alone. At the exact moment some of the beings believed that they were separate from that life force, the physical universe came into existence. At that instant the ego and mind were also created. Physical existence and time as we know it evolved in what seemed to be an instant. Time was not linear. Everything existed all at once in that single instant. I found myself slowly fading into the fabric of time. I felt profoundly sad and alone.

I again became aware of fragments of myself all over this universe. Slowly parts of me began to reassemble. Way off in the distance I could hear Miguel calling me back. It was difficult for me to find the way back. After what seemed like an eternity, I found myself back in the temple. I felt very disoriented and unsettled. Miguel was smiling at me with "that" smile. I feebly smiled back. We went around the room and shared our experiences as usual. When it was Miguel's turn he began to laugh. He looked at me and said I had made a little explosion. He said that we had been standing on a cliff together, and he had invited me to jump. I said sure, then we held hands and ran for the edge. When he looked back, I was still standing on the cliff shaking my head. He laughed and tried again to jump with me. After several more attempts, he said I finally jumped.

Miguel gestured for me to share my experience. I was still feeling very scattered and somewhat depressed. I haltingly told the group about the sensation of being fireworks and briefly shared some of my experiences. Miguel then asked me to teach class. I am still unsure what I spoke about. Miguel was going to San Francisco for a workshop, so class ended early.

When I left that night, I was very disoriented and confused. I felt as if I was only partially there. I drove home very slowly. The next day I was barely able to function, and I became concerned. That night I called Francisco. He said he knew what was going on so I had better come over. He explained to me that after an explosion, it would take weeks for all of my consciousness to return to my body. He worked on me energetically, and I felt less confused. We talked for a while, then I went home.

My sleep that night was very fitful because I kept dreaming about being in strange places. Ever since I was a child, I had felt like there was something missing. As my consciousness began to reassemble, I actually found a piece of myself that had been lost when I had died in the other initiation.

At times I laughed because I could sense parts of myself everywhere. I remembered the scene from *The Wizard of Oz* when the Scarecrow has his stuffing thrown all over by the flying monkeys. As he was lying there, he said something to the effect "That's me all over." I frequently felt like that over the ensuing weeks. As my consciousness began to reassemble I felt a sense of relief, yet I continued to be plagued by a sense of melancholy and depression. My melancholy continued to linger, until I went back and reviewed the creation scene again. The first time I viewed that scene, I had left feeling very disconnected. This time I realized that we were really still all one. After that my sense of loneliness disappeared.

I was very curious. I wanted to remember everything. I wanted to know exactly where I had gone and what I had done. I began to access information about my own past lives. I also developed the ability to put people in a trance and assist them in gaining access to their psyche, as well as their past lives. Miguel assured me that it would take years to access all the knowledge I had gathered in the experience. Even now, years later, I continue to access information that was gained in that experience.

As I shared my experience with some of the other apprentices, I was surprised at their reactions. Instead of being glad for me, some of them seemed angry or jealous. The advanced class had stopped meeting regularly some time ago. Ever since then, many of the students had split off into two small cliques. There was a great deal of competition and mistrust. Each group was intently trying to gain the most power. I had never participated in cliques, so I tried to maintain contact with both groups. I found myself studying alone with Miguel more often. I did not want to get lost in the endless quest for personal power.

EXERCISE THIRTEEN

Society supports us in strengthening our ego. I have found that true happiness and peace of mind are only achievable if you are willing to deflate the ego.

In order to defend our egos, we usually compare ourselves to others. The ego is constantly measuring its self-worth by judging others. Judgements limit your existence. Review your judgments. Observe yourself lovingly and compassionately. Remember, your personal power increases as you decrease your ego.

Do you have the need to be right or better than others?

What beliefs are you defending?

How do you view others?

Do you feel small and weak?

Do you ever put someone else down so you can feel better yourself?

Can you feel powerful without anger or without controlling others?

How do you feel about your body?

How do you feel about your social status?

Do you ever make decisions based on what "they" might think?

Do you have trouble speaking your truth?

How often do you connect with your spiritual center?

14

POWER

*There is a place within us that is at peace
no matter what is going on around us.*

 As my studies continued, I became painfully aware of the fact that many of my fellow students were beginning to be obsessed with gaining personal power. The original apprentices had gone their own way and most of them no longer came to the temple. Those who were left had all started long after I had. Miguel and I had several discussions about the responsibility of the teacher. I felt it was the teacher's responsibility to screen students and not teach people he or she felt would misuse the information. Miguel felt he should teach whoever came to him. Several of the newer students already appeared to be misusing their power. After a time, I too stopped going to the temple. I only studied with Miguel privately.

It was a harsh lesson for me. I saw people I cared about become lost in their pursuit of power. The saddest part was that they seemed to be losing their focus and their spiritual pursuits. The only thing that mattered was becoming more powerful. The whole process had accelerated when we finished the mirror room.

Miguel had often talked about how easy it was to gain power by using mirrors. With his original apprentices he had used four large mirrors. The apprentices would sit in a darkened room surrounded by the mirrors. They would place a candle at their feet and meditate with their eyes open. The effect was eerie. They would be able to see an infinite number of themselves reflected in the mirror. It was a very powerful and bizarre experience. Miguel and Francisco had built a small room in Miguel's backyard to be used as a mirror room.

One of the newer students was a dance instructor. She was sharing a space with a woman she no longer got along with. The walls were lined with mirrors. She told us the mirrors belonged to her and that she had every right to remove them. So one night we went over and took the mirrors off the walls. I later found out her claim that they were hers was questionable. Since I had worked with glass for years, I installed them in the room.

The first time I meditated in the room with Miguel, I was amazed. I rapidly traveled through time and space. As I sat there, I saw hundreds of images of myself looking back at me. They continued off into infinity, getting smaller and smaller. As I softly focused my attention on my images, one of them stepped out of the line and began to talk to me. It was a part of me that was still filled with emotional pain. I mentally communicated with it and assisted it in releasing the pain. I realized immediately what a wonderful tool this room could be.

It was decided that people would only be allowed to use the room with supervision. The problem with that was that there were only a few advanced students left. Before I knew it, students were pairing off into small groups and using the mirrors alone. The seductive nature of power immediately became evident. The mirrors allowed a person to gain great amounts of power, but that power was very dangerous when it wasn't properly channeled. The primary purpose of that power was to assist people in clearing out their emotional baggage so they could become clearer channels. When the power was filtered through the ego instead, the main result was chaos.

Each time Miguel and I used the mirror room, we had to clear it out because it was usually filled with a great deal of negativity. As I continued to clear out my old negative thought patterns, I began to get information about healing. I also continued to receive guidance on information that would assist people in releasing their old negative patterns. The other students were beginning to brag about being able to safely play in other universes. One of my closest friends began to exaggerate and frequently lie. I asked Miguel about all this, and he said it was all part of the students individual learning. He assured me he would not let things get out of hand. I felt I no longer belonged in the group at all, so I stopped going to most of the group functions.

My experience of working with power was very different than many of the other students. I had an intense fear of misusing the power. I was very conservative in my approach to using power, which was not really consistent with my personality. I was usually a risk taker. As I continued to work in the mirrors, I began to remember some of my past lives and realized why I wasn't tempted to misuse the power. In several of my past lives I had abused power badly, and I decided I didn't want to do that again. I saw power as something that was very sacred and that could be used as a bridge to connect me with my spiritual self.

Gaining power was a tricky business. I realized dealing with power was similar to retrieving a beach ball. If you are in the pool and lunge for a beach ball, it moves away rapidly. Instead if you approach the ball slowly and with caution, you can just reach out and grab it. I learned to approach power with a great deal of respect. I saw what it was doing to some of the other students, and I certainly didn't want to make the same mistakes.

I found that, for me, part of using power wisely was creating a sense of harmony with the universe. At times my ego would get in the way, and I would decide I wanted things my way. I could use my personal power to create things, but I always found that doing things my way was like swimming up stream— it was very tiring. Eventually I found that it is much easier to find out what the universe wants and do it that way, rather than struggle against the flow. The longer I studied, the more certain I became that my gifts were teaching and healing.

To my surprise, I found myself studying healing with Sister Sarita. Anyone watching must have had a great laugh. I still spoke no Spanish, and I was her assistant. I assumed someone would be there to translate. I was wrong. Most of her patients were also Mexican, so I was on my own. The first day I worked with her, she asked me to get her an egg. It must have taken us fifteen minutes of pantomime until I finally understand what she wanted. We laughed and managed to muddle through.

Sarita was a very holy woman and I learned to have a great deal of reverence for her use of power. I saw her heal ugly, oozing wounds on people with her touch and her love. I saw her give love freely to people of all types. I was moved to tears when she would do a blessing for people. She would light a candle and say a humble prayer to the Father to ask for help for those before her. Although I did not understand the words, I could feel the energy and I knew that it was powerful, gentle, and loving. I learned a lot from just being in Sarita's presence.

Miguel stressed power and competition, while Sarita stressed love and spirituality. My soul felt very much at home with Sarita and her husband. They had a very gentle and loving relationship. They usually seemed at ease and happy. I was always amused when Sarita would interact with Miguel. He was the youngest of her thirteen children, and she often treated him like a baby. At times I could see his impatience, yet their interactions were always loving. Sarita often expressed her displeasure with the unruliness of many of his students.

My first exposure to Miguel's and Sarita's healing abilities occurred early in my studies when I had slipped a disc in my back. I was in absolute agony. When the chiropractor couldn't help me, I went to see Miguel and he preformed psychic surgery. When he was done, he told me to get up off the table. I fully expected to experience severe pain. Much to my surprise there wasn't any pain. I was just a little stiff. He told me to come back in five days to have the stitches removed. For some reason I could accept psychic surgery but I had a hard time accepting psychic stitches. When I returned to have the stitches removed the stiffness went away. Before that I frequently had chronic pain in my lower back. After he worked on me I no longer did.

I slowly began to reassess some of my thoughts and feelings about power and its uses. While studying with Sarita, I realized once again how important my intentions and motives were. Both Miguel and Sarita worked with me so I could fine tune my healing skills. They showed me how to do psychic surgery. It was so intangible I had serious doubts about my ability. Miguel assured me that I was a very good healer. He told me that it was time for me to begin using my talents.

About that time I decided to go back to Vermont for a visit. Several friends of mine were having health problems, and they asked if I would work on them. I did and was shocked. I had never actually done psychic surgery, although Miguel continually assured me that I knew how to do it. While I was working on my friend's chest, I suddenly found my hand around her heart. I could feel it beating in my hand. My first reaction was to panic. I asked myself, what happens if she starts to bleed? I was immediately reminded that if she did, I would intuitively know how to stop it. Much to my surprise, her blocked arteries were perfectly clear after that.

The more I used my growing sense of personal power for others and for positive reasons, the more power I was able to access. My meditations were wonderful. Whenever I began to wonder about anything, I would begin getting information on it in my meditations. For a while I would wake up every day at three o'clock in the morning, go into the living room, and sit down in my meditation chair. A few minutes later I would begin to get reams of information on a variety of subjects. I felt like I was attending a lecture series. It was exciting and exhausting. I complained bitterly about waking up at that hour, but I missed it when it stopped.

I found the whole process of stalking and gaining power exciting. I could see why people so easily lost themselves in the process. At one point I clearly remember asking myself how I could control this power for my personal needs. Almost immediately my life fell apart, and I experienced a severe depression. I had briefly stepped into the world of pure ego and hated it.

It was a very exciting time in my studies. I felt like someone who had been unable to see for years and had been given back her sight. I was grateful and terrified at the same time. Emotional issues I thought I had handled came back to haunt me. Anything that stopped the flow of power became a liability, and I had to deal with it in some way.

I found myself spending more time alone. Nature began to communicate with me, especially the wind. I would find myself spending hours lost in contemplation. I was seldom sure where I had been or what I had been contemplating, but I felt very peaceful when I returned. Whenever I shared what was going on with Miguel, he seemed very pleased. I began to understand Miguel's methods a lot better. The best teacher about power was power itself. The lessons I had learned about power and my relationship to it were not easy for me to forget, but Miguel's warnings were. Some of the other students began to see their errors, while some became little Hitlers trying to control everyone and everything. I felt relieved when I noticed that their control was limited to people who wanted to be controlled.

One day I got a call to come to the temple for a special ceremony. When I arrived there, I learned that one of the students had been killed when the gas heater in her apartment had exploded. We all felt saddened, the mood inside the temple was somber. To my surprise, Miguel motioned for us to sit down and he began a formal class. For some time Miguel had been talking to me about power moves. He had told me they were another way to gain power. Tai Chi is an example of an ancient form of power moves. In power moves individuals allow the power to move their bodies. As they do so, their energy level will rise and over time they will be able to handle more power. It is a form of surrender to the harmony of the universe.

Once the class was assembled, he immediately began to talk about rituals and power moves. He talked about the Catholic Church and how many of the rituals had really been power moves. Originally priests had been men of power. Shamans and Naguals still were. In traditional religions, the leaders had become symbolic figureheads, rather than actually being able to channel power. A true person of power has the ability to look into the souls of others and assist them in their spiritual quests. That was what priest had done, but now most of the rituals had lost their true meaning. They were empty rituals rather than the sacred ceremonies originally designed to channel power.

Miguel talked about ceremonies and how they could be used in many different ways. As we begin to look at our everyday lives, we can see that there are many ceremonies that have simply lost their meaning. Weddings, graduations, funerals, and baptisms are all examples of ceremonies that have lost much of their original meaning and power. People often participate in those ceremonies without much regard for their true meaning. As Miguel spoke, I began to get mental images of the beauty and power of those ceremonies when they were preformed as sacred acts.

My attention returned to the class when I heard Miguel beginning to discuss the true meaning of an invocation. He said that a invocation was one of the most powerful ceremonies there was. It was a ceremony during which the powers of the universe and creation were called upon and directed for a specific purpose. The person actually invoked those powers and then used them. He went on to say that an invocation was one of the most solemn ceremonies and should be used with a great deal of discretion. In a person's lifetime, there may be only one occasion that would call for the use of a true invocation.

An invocation combined the use of the spoken word along with power movements. Miguel described the precise movements needed in order to perform this ceremony. He warned us to be certain before we ever decided to use this ceremony. He had all the students stand around him in a circle and practice the power moves for the ceremony. We stopped before we completed the final gesture. Even though we didn't complete the movements, you could feel the power building in the room. My skin tingled from being in the presence of so much power.

Miguel had us go through the ceremony one last time and, unknown to any of us in the room, he used our energy and completed the ceremony. His intention was to send the energy to the woman who had just died. He wanted to assist her on her journey home. When people die, it takes them a while to lose their human form or remember that they are pure spirit. Miguel felt that by using the energy of the invocation, he could shorten that time. None of us knew that she was still barely alive. She was actually in the process of leaving her body. Since Miguel didn't know she was still alive, he didn't protect her body. So instead of dying, she was revived.

The next day when Miguel found out, he immediately went to see her. She was in terrible pain. Her body was covered with burns, and she had no chance of surviving. When Miguel talked to her, she remembered being out of her body. She was relieved that the struggle was over. She saw the group and Miguel as she was moving towards the light. Suddenly she saw a lightning bolt flow into her body, and she was drawn back into it immediately. A few days later she finally died.

Almost immediately Miguel became very ill. He was near death. He said that it was payment for his misuse of power. One of the most important rules when using power was never to interfere with someone else's evolutionary process. He had changed that woman's path by the use of his power. Rather than carry the karma, he chose to get ill in order to let go of it. I was confused because it looked like punishment to me. Miguel assured me that it wasn't and that his illness was part of his learning.

On occasions I had seen people suffering and wanted to reach out and heal them. I had always resisted the temptation, now I understood why. The more I observed people and the use of power, the more I realized the importance of prudence. I decided I would allow my heart or my spiritual center to be my guide, and as much as possible stay out of my ego and my head. I would rather make a mistake by not using my power when it might have been appropriate than to misuse it in any way.

Exercise Fourteen

I believe all human beings can access healing energy.
vidual does not perform the healing, they merely act as ʜan-
nel for healing energy. The more thoroughly the healer can "get
out of the way," the more effective they are as a channel. It is
important to let go of the ego as much as possible and step into
the heart. The ego blocks healing energy.

You can begin practicing these techniques with a friend's
assistance. You can each take turns practicing to be a channel for
healing energy.

First stand quietly behind the person and close your eyes.
Focus your attention on your breathing and relax. As much as
possible let go of your mind and step into your spiritual center.
Imagine standing in the presence of a being of light who is a
healer. Mentally ask the being of light to help you.

Imagine yourself opening up to receive the energy. Practice
feeling the energy flowing over and through you. Imagine that
you are standing in a waterfall and let yourself feel the energy
pouring over you. As long as you intend to channel this energy,
you are, even if your mind doubts your ability. The energy is
always present; it flows with our intentions.

Next feel the energy flowing out through your hands. Allow
yours hands to be intuitively guided and just allow the energy to
flow. Imagine yourself cleaning this person's energy field. This
energy is one of pure love, so just stroke the person's energy
field lovingly. When you are done, stand behind the person and
silently give thanks for being used as a channel. Then wash your
hands in running water to release any impurities you picked up.

What are your beliefs about healing?

How do you feel about Western medicine?

How do you feel about alternative healing methods?

How do you feel about yourself when you get sick? Do you feel like you have failed in some way?

15

MEDICINE WOMAN

*Walk in humility, live in love,
and know true joy.*

 As my studies continued, I found myself spending more and more time alone with Miguel. I seldom saw any of the other students. The few I had felt comfortable with had left the area or were no longer in contact with me or the group. I had an uneasy feeling that I would be the next to leave. More and more my studies were being directed by my meditations and the beings I contacted there. I loved the wind, I could feel it caress and comfort me whenever I felt alone. Although it never spoke in words, it talked to me. Miguel seemed increasingly distant.

One day Miguel called me and said it was time for him to do a ceremony for me. I was shocked because in all the years I had known him, he had never called me. He told me to bring a stick, some feathers, a crystal, some red cloth, a red robe, and a leather hide. I asked him why, and he laughed and told me to bring them to his house the following evening.

As I approached his house, I had no idea what to expect. I was very surprised to find the house empty except for the two of us. The night was very dark and still. We went out into the yard, and he had me sit in the same spot the fire had been during the Fire Initiation. He looked at the things I had brought and smiled at everything with approval, except for my stick. He immediately got up and began to look around the yard for another one. Finally he found one that suited him and again sat down in front of me.

Miguel placed a candle in the center of the circle. As he sat there he was very intense. Slowly he began to cut the red cloth into narrow strips. His attention was totally focused as he laid everything out in front of me. I sat facing the east with my red robe on. Slowly and methodically Miguel wound the red strips around the stick until it was totally covered. Then he attached several feathers to the end of the stick. I had also brought a large crystal cluster. He picked it up and began running it through the candle flame while he began to chant. He called upon the powers of the universe and upon the powers of the four directions. He called upon the earth, the wind, the sun, and the rain. He asked each of them to bless and guide me.

Slowly he began to channel power to me. I realized this would be my final initiation. He did a ceremony of consecration which made me a holy woman. He went into trance and the ceremony continued. He began to talk about the powers of nature and told me I had a special gift. I had been blessed by the spirits of nature. The wind had agreed to be my ally. It would always allow me to use its power and healing nature. The wind would carry messages to me and heal my soul. I was very moved as he spoke. I had felt a real affinity for the wind, now I knew why.

He talked about my path as a teacher and a healer. He said that I was a Medicine Woman and my gifts were many and varied. I had come to teach others and to remind them who they really are. He told me to always use my power wisely and to always follow my heart. He told me my life would be about great change. I was a traveler and would be a guide to many. I had come to teach love and help people heal their hearts and spirits. As I listened to Miguel's words my first thought was, "I can't do all that." I took a deep breath and tried to focus on the ceremony.

Miguel stood up in front of me and asked me to do the same. He asked me what I was willing to give in exchange for the power. My voice seemed to come from behind me as I pledged to do my best to be of service to the Great Spirit. I thanked the universe for the gifts and asked to be of service to humanity. I told the universe that I felt inadequate for the task and asked for the wisdom and strength to complete my mission. Gently and slowly the wind began to swirl around me. The night had been totally still, but now the wind began to gently caress me. I felt the wind go right through me. It touched me with tenderness. I felt loved and filled with power.

Miguel held his hands up over his head and called upon the universe. He said, "Behold, here stands a woman of power and she comes from the east." I stood there and looked up at the stars and listened to the wind. I breathed deeply and allowed my body to be filled with power. Then I took a step forward and said out loud, "I am a woman of power and I come from the east." At that instant the wind extinguished the candle, and the ceremony was over. Miguel embraced me and we went inside.

We chatted for a while, then I decided it was time for me to go home. I felt a sense of sadness as I left the house. At some level I knew that I was no longer a student and it was time for me to go off on my own. I tried to dismiss my sadness as the usual let down after a ceremony. I had never expected Miguel to make me a Medicine Woman. I felt honored and somewhat confused.

The following day I had a sense of elation which was very different from my reaction to the other ceremonies. The phrase, "I am a woman of power and I come from the east," kept running through my mind. I found myself drawn to the desert. I had lived near the edge of the desert for several years, but I had gone there only once or twice. Now I felt compelled to go there. My birthday was a few weeks off, so I decided to do a ceremony for myself. I decided that I wanted to be on top of a mountain at the hour of my birth. I planned on doing a ceremony in which I would asked the universe for its blessing for the coming year.

I asked a friend of mine, who was also one of my students, to come with me. We began the drive out to the mountains in silence. On the way up, we skirted the desert. At one point as we were winding our way up the mountain, we came to a place that overlooked the Painted Desert. The view was spectacular. We drove on. When we had gone about a mile I instructed my friend to turn around. We stopped in a parking area at the base of a steep cliff. There was a winding path up the side of the cliff. It was very hot and there was no wind. We slowly began to ascend, and I began to talk about Paramahansa Yogananda's death. When he died, he had just finished talking and stepped gently out of his body. His body had not decayed, even though it wasn't embalmed. I am not sure why I talked about that.

We were walking along side by side. Suddenly I fell silent and felt myself entering an altered state. As I continued up the cliff, I realized I was alone. When I looked back, I saw my friend standing motionless below me. I hesitated for a moment and then continued up the mountain. The wind began to swirl around me as I reached the top. A moment before there hadn't been a thing stirring. I sat down on an outcropping of rocks that seemed suspended in space. The view was absolutely spectacular. The desert was spread out below me, and I immediately felt the power of this place surge through me. I knew instantly that this was a very sacred place. I thanked it for calling to me and welcoming me.

The easiest way I can describe the experience is to say that I began to communicate with the desert and the mountain. I asked for its blessing, and it asked my intentions and for my allegiance. I was deeply moved by the beauty and power of this place. I felt loved, accepted, and totally energized. I had never experienced anything like it. The whole time I sat on that outcropping, the wind howled around me. It seemed like I had been there just a few moments when the wind suddenly stopped. I knew it was time for me to return to the world. I thanked the spirits of this place and asked if I could return. Momentarily the wind picked up again, which I decided meant yes.

When I walked down to rejoin my friend, she looked relieved to see me coming. When we got back to the car, I realized that I had been up there for over an hour. I asked her why she had stopped, and she said that she had encountered a wall. She had been unable physically to proceed any further. She said that I had disappeared into a rainbow of colors and her first fear had been that I had crossed over to the other side. She said she thought that, since I had told her about Yogananda's death, I had been preparing her for my own death. She said that most of the time I had been gone, she had been trying to decide how she was going to explain my disappearance. We both laughed hardily and continued our drive up to the mountains.

I did find myself frequently returning to that place on the side of the cliff. I was always amazed. I would begin to feel compelled to go there, and a few days later I would find myself driving there. It was a very special place to me. I felt the presence of the Great Spirit there. As soon as I began to walk up the path, I always experienced a sense of oneness and power.

I was always alone by the time I reached my sacred place. Once, as I began my hike up the path, I was disappointed to see another hiker up ahead of me on the trail. To my surprise, he suddenly stopped a few feet in front of me. He was at the very place my friend had been compelled to stop. I walked by him, went to my spot, and sat there for at least an hour. He stood still as if he were transfixed. When I walked back down past him, he turned and smiled. Then he walked on as if nothing had happened.

Amazingly we reached the top of the mountain a few minutes prior to the time of my birth. I had brought a candle and a letter I was going to read to the universe. My friend sat opposite me on a large rock. The wind cooperated and the candle remained burning. We both went into a meditation, then I called upon the spirits of the mountain to assist me. A huge owl flew overhead and its shadow passed over both of us. Instead of reading the letter I had written, I decided to ask the universe to help me release whatever stood in my way. I told the universe that I wanted to experience my oneness with the Great Spirit.

We went to a nearby town that was well known for its apple pies. We wandered around, ate pie, and played tourists. It was a gorgeous fall day. The leaves were beginning to turn colors, the air was so clear and crisp. My life was beginning to take on a more gentle quality. The day seemed very relaxed and peaceful. I loved being alive. I certainly had come a long way from the person who was a drug addict and had tried to kill herself.

Several months later I asked Miguel if he would like to go whale watching. We met at the dock and boarded a huge sail boat. I had not seen him for quite a while so I was very glad to see him. The air was very brisk and we huddled close together. Miguel always seemed happy and relaxed no matter what was going on around him. I seldom saw him in a setting that didn't entail him being the teacher. It seemed strange to be just playing with him. He went up to the bar and got a beer. We sat and talked. I was enjoying the wind and the sun.

As soon as we reached the open water whales were spotted. Everyone got very excited as we cautiously approached the whales. Miguel had an impish smile on his face. I asked him if he had called the whales, and he smiled. The captain was telling us why we could only go within so many feet of the whales. Besides being against the law, he said that if we approached any closer we might scare the whales. He was beginning to complain about a small vessel that was much too close to the whales when a whale surfaced directly under our boat. Its eye was right below the spot Miguel and I were sitting. It seemed to look directly into my soul and as I looked into its eye, I honored the spirit I saw there. The moment was awesome. The captain was panicking because he was clearly too close to the whales. When the whale dove down, I sat there and laughed.

The show the whales put on for us was amazing. I had brought my camera and got wonderful shots of tail fins and a mother with her calf. The day was magical. I had been whale watching many times but had never actually seen whales that close before. The sun began to set as we sailed back towards shore. Miguel looked very serious and told me that we needed to talk. He said that he had taught me all he could. He was finished as my teacher. He told me it was time for me to go off on my own and teach in my own way. I was shocked and began to argue with him. I told him that I still had a lot to learn from him.

Miguel smiled and told me that my formal studies with him were finished. He said that I only remembered a fraction of what I had learned. Most of my knowledge was still locked away in my memory banks. I had gathered most of my knowledge on the ethereal level, so it would take me time to remember it. He told me that it was very important for me to begin teaching others. He told me that my students would push me to remember. At times people would ask me questions and I would not know the answers until they came out of my mouth.

The ship docked and we went ashore. I lingered for a few moments and talked to Miguel. He gave me a kiss and then left. I felt very sad and scared. I was sure that I didn't know anything. I felt like a little kid that had lost her parents at an amusement park. As I approached my exit on the freeway, the lights began to come on and I was reminded of all the nights I had returned from class filled with excitement or fear. I knew in my heart those days were over. Within a few days some people approached me about becoming apprentices, the circle continued.

EXERCISE FIFTEEN

The wind has always been an important part of my studies. As soon as I feel the wind, I immediately focus my attention on the moment. Spend some time out in nature. Allow yourself to feel and experience the elements with your senses, not your mind. Find a comfortable spot and immerse yourself in feeling the elements. Relax and allow yourself to get in touch with your body. Slow your mind down and turn your attention to your senses.

Spend some time each day just feeling the elements until they begin to "talk" to you. Mother Nature can be a wonderful teacher if we are willing to listen. Spend some time getting familiar with the elements.

Where do the wind and sun touch you?

Does their touch feel loving or harsh?

Are you comfortable focusing on the elements?

Focus your attention on your skin and the layers of flesh below it. How does it feel?

How does it feel to focus your attention on your body rather then your mind?

So often the only time we notice our bodies is if they are malfunctioning. If you are in pain, you are aware of your body; if you're not, you probably live in your head most of the time. Spend some time getting to know your body. Sit naked in front of a mirror and observe your body.

How do you feel about your body?

Are there any parts of your body you dislike? Try loving those parts.

Do you experience pain in any area of your body?

If you do experience pain, talk to your body. What does it say to you?

What messages does the pain have for you?

What is your body trying to tell you?

16

THE CIRCLE

Find your spiritual center, live from it, love,
keep your heart open, walk softly, and laugh joyously.

 Several students in my healing class approached me about becoming my apprentices. They had often listened to me share stories about my studies and wanted to learn in the traditional manner also. I debated about it for several days. I hesitated because I wasn't sure the traditional way was my way. One day while I was debating, I remembered my promise to teach at least seven more. I decided I could teach in the traditional manner and use my personal perspective. I told the people I would meet with them and discuss it.

The first thing I did was ask them why they wanted to study with me. I made it clear I would only teach people if they were serious and wanted the knowledge to expand their spirituality, not their ego. They were a wonderful group of people, very loving and gentle, so the teachings began.

The first night the classes formally began I sat in my living room and smiled. This sure was a long way from my origins as a New York City street kid. I never dreamt I would be sitting in a house on the beach in California teaching people how to access other realms of consciousness and talking about spirituality.

I learned so much by teaching those people. I learned about love, acceptance, joy, and sharing. I found that in order to teach, I had to share the real me. I could not hide behind the mask I had learned to present to the world. I had to show people the inner me. I couldn't hide behind my walls and be effective as a teacher. I always looked forward to the classes. There was always a lot of love, sharing, and laughter. Sometimes I felt inadequate because I wasn't at all sure if I really knew the answers until they came out of my mouth. It was an exciting time for both the students and myself. In a sense we became a family.

I continued to see Miguel sporadically. I told him about my group and he was glad. One night I asked him to come and talk to the group. I was amused at their reaction, they were terrified about meeting him. He had recently been married and his wife sat in the corner and took notes. The evening went quite nicely and no one died of fright. They all told me they were glad that they had finally met him.

We spent a lot of time on the beach meditating. One day as we sat there, I called up death for them. The sun was almost setting and there was a long, red shadow on the water. It looked like a shaft of light aimed at their hearts. I told them to focus their attention on the horizon and asked if they felt a presence there. I felt like I was in a time machine and saw myself the first time Miguel did that for me. Their bodies all recoiled with fear.

They had the same reaction I once had, terror. I was amazed because what I was seeing now was a very gentle, loving energy that was a wonderful teacher. Death constantly walks along with us, reminding us that we are mortal. When we do die, I realized that death is there as a gentle guide that lovingly helps us shed our body. I no longer feared this teacher. When I tried to tell my students that, they just wanted to go inside.

As I began sharing my knowledge in the way in which I had been taught, I was able to view the lessons from a different perspective. Miguel had often said that the students push the teacher to learn, now I understood what he meant by that statement. The lessons were so much clearer, and my perspective so much more loving and gentle without the fear. As a student, I had experienced fear so often that I had missed a lot of the excitement and joy in the teachings. My time as a student had seemed so serious and heavy. Now I realized that my experience was totally due to my perspective.

My life began to open up and expand in amazing ways. One day as I was walking on the beach surrendering myself to the wind, I found myself standing out on the ocean. I was startled and immediately found myself standing on the beach again. I realized I could experience someone else's reality by focusing my attention on him or her. I could literally walk in another person's shoes. I found myself experiencing compassion instead of judging others.

I found that the wind was a powerful ally. I can't even begin to describe its effect on me. At times I would sit on the beach and allow the wind to blow through my body. I would ask it to remove any blocks or negativity and afterwards I would feel relaxed and at peace. Whenever I felt the wind I was able to change my focus. If I felt alone and I focused my attention on the wind, I could feel the love in its presence. It always told me when it was time to come back. It was always around when I performed ceremonies.

My external life also began to change dramatically. I had not been in an intimate relationship for years and became involved in one. It was glorious although short-lived. I was able to face my fears of intimacy because of that experience. I also realized that it was almost time for me to move on. My students began to progress very rapidly. Before I knew, it was time for their Water Initiation. The ceremony was wonderful. We walked down the beach and went out to a point were the rocks jutted out into the ocean. There was a little flat rock that I sat on and each student in turn waded out and sat opposite me. I did a ceremony for each one, and as I completed the ceremony a large wave would come in and wash over both of us. A pod of dolphins was swimming offshore just a short distance away. They seemed to be blessing our endeavors.

After the initiation, one of the students left the group. The other students were saddened, but his fear spoke louder than his desire for knowledge. We spent a lot of time talking and learning together. I watched them go through the same emotional turmoil I had. Since I was a somewhat dispassionate observer, I could see that the real struggle was between their heads and their hearts. I remembered Miguel telling me this path was a battle between our spiritual self and our minds, or our "computers." I saw that struggle very clearly. Their fear of losing control would force them to make decisions that created more stress in their lives, which would cause more fear and on and on.

Slowly, as I watched their struggle, I began to trust my process more and more. I saw time and again how my life took on a sense of ease and magic when I surrendered to what was happening in my life, rather than trying to control it. When my relationship suddenly ended, I was initially frustrated and sad. Once I was able to let the relationship go, I saw how necessary the ending had been. I couldn't have gotten my needs met in that relationship, and it was almost time for me to leave California. If I had stayed in that relationship, I would have missed out on all the adventures I have had in Hawaii.

It was easier for me to see how my students caused much of their own pain and internal turmoil. I could easily see how their resistance about looking at their emotional issues and limiting beliefs caused most of their pain. In the past I had believed my pain had come from the events in my life. But as I watched my students, I began to realize more fully that most of the pain actually came from our resistance to change. I became more willing to relax and let life happen rather then trying to anticipate and control what was going to happen next. I began to see how life could actually be fun. As soon as I stepped into the flow of the universe and let go of my limited perspectives, life became easy.

I had wanted to move to Hawaii for years, and I felt that it was time. I decided that I would move as soon as my students had completed the Fire Initiation. I loved my little place at the beach. I had recently bought a cruiser bike with the fat wheels and no gears. I really enjoyed going for a ride on the board walk at sunset. My mind told me to stay, but I knew in my heart that it was time to go. I was excited about moving, but I was also sad. I had really enjoyed my life here. My students were very nervous about me leaving. They didn't want me to go. I meditated a lot and as much as possible tried to let go of my desire to control things.

I frequently went up to the mountains to visit my sacred spot. I thought of taking my class up there, but the time never seemed to be right. At times I felt like the universe had put my life on fast forward, at other times I felt like everything was going at a snail's pace. I wrote a book about my counseling methods during this time period. I had never imagined myself writing a book. I was amazed that I was able to do so with such little effort. I felt myself slowly detaching from California.

Before I knew it, my students were ready for the Fire Initiation. I tried to get in touch with Miguel. I thought it would be nice if he attended. Much to my surprise he had gone back to Mexico. No one was really sure where in Mexico. The best answer I could get was that he was somewhere in the interior of Mexico which is a rather large area. I was sad he hadn't said goodbye and I wouldn't be able to tell him where I was moving.

We had the Fire Initiation on the beach late one night. When I looked up at the cliffs, they were filled with people silently watching. It was both eerie and magical. During the ceremony, I made one of the students the leader of the band. He was very wise and could teach them a lot if they listened. He was sure that he didn't know anything. I told him that the answers would come. Much of my teachings seemed like déjà vu. I often had the feeling that life was an endless circle of events and knowledge being repeated in slightly different ways.

I got caught up in the endless cycle of activity necessary to plan such a big move. The classes continued to meet, and I looked forward to our gathering in my small place each week.

Several of the students had dropped out after the Fire Initiation. There was a growing sense of excitement and fear of loss. Each week we shared our emotions, hopes, and dreams. I talked a lot about living from our spiritual center and releasing our need to control. I had begun to see how ludicrous my desire to control really was. First of all, my perspective was too limited to see the whole picture and second, I couldn't control things anyway.

Before I knew it, the day of my departure had arrived. Class met as usual. I was so scattered they had to help me pack my bags. When they arrived, I was in the process of doing my laundry and it was clear I needed another suitcase. I stepped outside to get my laundry and a neighbor offered to give me another suitcase. When I returned with the suitcase they looked at me with surprise. I think that for the moment they believed that I had conjured it up. It was a bittersweet night. We did a ceremony for closure. During it each person had the opportunity to say what our time together had meant to them, as well as express his or her feelings about this parting. The goodbyes were difficult. The class made plans to continue meeting. The next day I went to the airport with my belongings and my dog.

As my plane approached Hawaii, I heard or felt the islands welcoming me. I had left the past behind and was moving into a new life. For once in my life I knew I was moving towards something, rather then running away from the past. I spent the next few years setting up my counseling practice and getting settled in the islands. I all but forgot my work with Miguel. For a time I had sent tapes back to the students, but then the class had stopped meeting. I was teaching workshops and classes about emotional healing and seldom used my healing skills. My main emphasis was still finding that spiritual center, but I seldom spoke about Miguel.

When I first arrived in Hawaii I had a hard time meditating. My mind was so concerned with everyday life that I lost my connection with my spiritual center for a time. I became so worried about finding a place to live that I forgot who I was and what life was really about. One day the wind began to talk to me again and I began to remember. I had forgotten to trust life and to have fun. I found a place to live, got a job, and started enjoying life again. Sometime later I started doing workshops on the beach. I found that if I touched people while I was working with them they accessed their emotions much more easily. I found myself talking more and more about Miguel. I began to get more in touch with the traditional ways.

I moved to the beach again and immediately began to connect again with the elements and myself. People began to ask me about my teachings. My meditations again became a fountain of information. I frequently talked about my studies with "the Shaman." My counseling and teaching practice began to take on a whole new dimension.

One weekend I decided to do a two-day workshop on the beach at my house. It rained all day Saturday which was unusual for Hawaii at that time of year. We spent the entire day inside writing and processing. Everyone got clear about what they wanted to release from their lives. I began to talk about energy and ceremonies. I talked about my studies with Miguel and about releasing control and surrendering to our spiritual center.

Sunday the sun shone brightly and we spent most of the day on the beach working with the elements. I had people doing exercises I hadn't thought about in years. I had the participants find their power spot on the beach. I was reminded of my students back in California fidgeting all over the beach, trying to find just the right spot. I encouraged people to begin to explore their spiritual center and to connect with the essence of who and what they really are. I guided them in a meditation in which they connected with themselves and that sense of oneness with the universe. After that I had them get clear about what they wanted to begin experiencing in their lives.

At the end of the day I started a fire on the beach to burn our writings. We did a simple ceremony in which the participants declared out loud to the universe what they were releasing and what they wanted to experience instead. I watched their faces soften and change. It was a magical experience. At the end of the ceremony I found myself standing at the head of the group. I said "I am a woman of power and I come from the east." A few weeks later I started this book. The circle was complete.

EXERCISE SIXTEEN

You could look for a group who is teaching about spirituality and healing. Or you might form your own group. Find some people you like and trust and spend time exploring your spirituality together. Enjoy life and, above all else, have fun.

Hopefully as you have read this book your thoughts about life have changed. Answer the following questions and compare them with your answers to the questions in Chapter One.

How do you view your world?

Are you an important part of your world or do you feel separate?

Is it a safe place or is it hostile?

What is your role, are you the hero or the victim?

How does it work, is it random or preordained?

How have your answers to these questions changed?

What has changed for you as you read this book?

What would you like to change right now?

My Story

I was born in the fall of 1949, after a very long, hot summer in New York City. When it is hot in New York City—it is hot! The heat seems to radiate off the buildings and the pavement. Even the asphalt melts. My parents lived in a small walk up flat in Queens. My mother said it was so hot the year I was born that she would put the fan in the refrigerator and sit in front of it to try to cool off.

When it was time for me to be born, I must have changed my mind about coming out. My mother was in labor for three days and they finally pulled me out with forceps. I have a mental image of myself sitting in the womb and saying to the universe "I am just fine in here thank you. I think I've made a terrible mistake and I am not coming out." I cried a lot as a baby and drove one of the neighbors so crazy that he would pound on the wall. My father would get even by jamming the picture on the man's TV set with a generator he borrowed from work.

Evidently I also drove my mother crazy, she developed post-partum psychosis. As a child I always had nightmares of horribly distorted faces coming at me. I found out about my mother's illness in my thirties and finally understood the dreams. I was reliving my mother's insanity.

I was a bright child with very strong ideas about what I wanted and what I didn't want. I had blonde curly hair, big blue eyes, and an impish grin. I looked like a little fairy princess. I now know I was special and lovable. But as a child I knew that there was something seriously wrong with me, that I was a bad girl. As a toddler strangers were always coming over and patting my head and saying I was cute. I hated being touched. One day when an old man patted my head, I hit him and told him to cut it out. My mother was horrified and let me know just how rude I had been.

Today I know that my mother had been terribly abused by her mother, so she had a very poor self-image. Her "okayness" was defined by my behavior. If I wasn't perfect she looked bad.

Back then I was a small child that desperately wanted to be loved and accepted. I had a very strong personality, I was gentle, loving, very sensitive, and extremely smart. If I didn't understand the reason for doing something or I didn't agree with the reason I would do it my way. The combination of my personality and my parents' lack of self-esteem created a great deal of emotional pain. I learned at an early age that if I was to receive the love and acceptance I wanted, I would have to become someone else.

I seemed to have the uncanny ability to embarrass my mother. When I was five or six we were walking down one of the avenues in Manhattan. I had a little voice that could carry for blocks. As we stood at the corner waiting for the light to change, a group of nuns arrived. I had never seen nuns before, but I had been to the zoo. I looked over and in my best little girl voice I looked at my mother and said, "Ma, look at all the penguins." As I recall the nuns laughed, my mom wanted to die, kill me, or both. My uniqueness was not appreciated that day or most days for that matter.

We moved to Yonkers, which borders on the Bronx. The neighborhood children were all boys. At first we were all young enough that my sex didn't matter, but eventually the boys remembered that they hated little girls and refused to play with me. I remember feeling different and I always felt like I didn't belong. I was always getting in fights and coming home bloody and bruised. My mom taught me how to fight dirty and after that I could give as well as receive. When I would come home bloody, my mom would stand me up and tell me not to cry. Her standard response was that the wound was a long way from my head and I didn't sit on it, so it was no big deal. She also told me that there would never be anyone there for me, so I had better learn to be strong now.

I never felt like I belonged anywhere. I can remember walking home at dusk looking in other people's windows. I had overwhelming feelings of loneliness and longing. I would look at the warm, yellow glow coming from their windows and know something was missing in my life. I felt like everyone else knew how to play the game of life, except me. They had something I didn't have and I wanted it. I spent years trying to figure out what "it" was. The only thing I was certain of was "it" was outside of myself.

My family life was very chaotic. My mother used amphetamines for years to control her weight. Both my parents drank heavily. I was never sure where I stood or what the rules were on any given day. I was not given the opportunity to develop a true sense of who I was. I was too busy trying to figure out how to act so I could fit into their world. When people would ask me what I wanted to do or be, I was never sure how to answer because the concept of "me" was totally foreign. I only knew how to define myself in terms of other people.

I learned very early that if I showed my emotions, I was often ridiculed. After a time I was no longer able to acknowledge them, even to myself. I began to view my sensitivity as a flaw. I'd get furious at myself if I wanted to cry. If I did cry, I made sure no one else was around. My sense of isolation from myself and the world continued to grow. I read a lot and began to feel like one of the victims in a Dickens novel, except I knew no one would ever save me.

When I was a young child, my parents made me go to church alone. For a time I was in the choir and went to the early services. There was a beautiful rosette stained glass window in front of the choir loft. The sun would stream through the window during the service. I was fascinated by the light and the shadows the window created. I would often miss the cue to stand up and sing because my attention was so focused on the window. One day I came home from church all upset. The minister had given a hell-fire and brimstone sermon and I was terrified that I was going to hell. My hunch is my father told me not to worry, but what I heard for some reason was that there was no God or that God didn't care about me.

I spent most of my time in my own world. My imagination was very active, and I would often "go someplace else" while I was in school. In fifth grade we had desks with drawers underneath them. One day I went into my drawer to get something and it must have made an interesting noise. I began to beat on it like a drum. I was having a great time when suddenly I "came back," to find the teacher standing over me and the entire class laughing hysterically. I was mortified. The teacher assumed I was doing it on purpose. When I was sent to the principal's office one more time, I didn't have the words to tell him what was really going on. I couldn't say I was bored with school. I couldn't say I couldn't sleep at night because I was so afraid, of what, I didn't know. I had no way to express my feelings because no one ever told me feelings were ok. I was reprimanded and another "she is uncooperative" comment went into my file.

Part of my family's legacy was my inability to talk about or even acknowledge what was going on with me. I was always fine. No one ever told me to tell the truth—what was really true for me. I learned at a very early age to tell people what I thought they wanted to hear. Forget the truth. Both my parents had been raised in abusive families, but they were unable to admit that to themselves so we continued telling the family lie. To people on the outside our family looked wonderful. As an only child it was pure hell. I was either alone or around adults. I had no one to show me how to interact with my peers. I grew up believing that I was a victim, bad, inadequate, and just generally unlovable and ineffective. I never had words for how I was feeling, and I didn't know I could ask for help. My parents were so filled with suppressed rage that I was frightened most of the time.

In seventh grade I was put in the disciplinary section of my class. I was certain they had made a terrible mistake. These kids were mean and angry. I was terrified, but then I put on my "I don't care" routine. The girl that was the leader of one of the toughest gangs in the school was made my locker partner. Linda put up her photographs on my side of the locker so I took them down. She challenged me to a fight, I accepted. I figured I would show up, take my lumps and be done with the whole thing. At first Linda was doing a good job of beating me up, and I was just waiting for it to be over. Then she made the mistake of hitting my head on the pavement. I lost my temper and beat her up. Finally her brother broke up the fight and literally kicked her all the way down the street.

The next day at school I saw Linda and her gang hanging out at the bottom of the stairs. I knew I was going to be killed when I reached the bottom, but I was too cool to run. When I got to the bottom, her second in charge put her arm around me. I knew I was going to be knifed. Instead I was informed that I was now the leader. I said thanks but no thanks. After that Linda was my guardian angel. No one dared to bother me because they would have to answer to her.

That year I also decided I wanted to join the chorus. I was in the band and really loved music. My music teacher Miss Pinto was not very fond of me. The feeling was mutual. When I signed up she let all the other kids audition together, she made me do it in class in front of everyone. I was very embarrassed by that so, of course, I decided that it was necessary to get even. For the next few weeks I drove the woman crazy. One day I brought her a bouquet of dandelions, which we also called "pee in the beds" because if you receive a bunch of them you are supposed to pee in your bed. I gave them to her at the start of class and explained their magical powers. She was not amused, so it was off to the principal's office again. I was suspended from school on a fairly regular basis, but my mom always managed to fix it for me.

In ninth grade my father moved my mother and me to a rural town in Vermont. He intended to move with us, but wasn't able to come until years later. My mother hated the country. I had enjoyed visiting Vermont in the summer, but living there was another matter. I had just gotten my New York City street-kid act down, these country kids looked at me like I had horns. When I first moved there they would call me over and tell me to talk. They loved to laugh at my New York accent. I got rid of my accent fast. I no longer knew who I was, so I tried to be who I thought everyone else wanted me to be. I spent most of my energy trying to figure out how to fit in. It never occurred to me to ask myself what I wanted.

One weekend a friend of mine from New York came to visit. She was pretty and could interact well with boys. I was over-weight and had no idea how to play the dating game, or even if I wanted to. She met two boys from Canada who took us out to a bar. I ordered a drink and to my surprise they served me. I had a few drinks and a miracle occurred. That switch in my head that was attached to the voice that told me I didn't belong any-where shut off. I experienced a sense of belonging, it was magic. For the first time in my life I felt like I was alive and acceptable.

When I was 16 I got my first car. I drank heavily through most of high school, it made it a lot easier to suppress those pesky feelings. I began actively running away from who I was. I also began feeling a sense of remorse about who I was becoming.

I remember sitting by my window one night watching a violent lightning storm. The beauty and power of the storm was magnificent. Each time the lightning struck, the mountains would just come alive. The whole room would vibrate with the thunder. I had a sense of longing deep within my very being. I knew something was missing in my life. Now I realize that what was missing in my life was my connection with that beauty. I was no longer connected with myself, my heart, or my world. I felt my spirit stirring that night, but I had no idea I even had a spirit. It took me years to find out what that longing really was.

The day after Christmas when I was a senior in high school, our house burned to the ground. We weren't able to save anything. I had been made a ski instructor that day, so I came home all excited. I wanted to tell my parents the good news. I was devastated. I had grown to love that house. From that day on my belief that, "whenever something good happened, something bad would happen," was carved in stone. Becoming a ski instructor was the first thing I had accomplished that was important to me. At some level I decided that I would no longer get attached to things and I would no longer do things for myself. I knew that the fire was somehow my fault. If I had just...the house wouldn't have burned.

By now I was battling serious bouts of depression. I was beginning to believe that whatever I got attached to would be taken away. I lacked a true sense of who I was or what I wanted. I was absolutely certain that my happiness resided outside myself. Happiness was something I tried to find for years. It never occurred to me to ask myself what I enjoyed doing.

I had begun to believe that I was responsible for almost everything that happened in my world. I felt responsible for the way others felt, how they acted, and anything else that happened. I was sure that it was all my fault. I also believed I was powerless to change anything. When I first began reading metaphysical literature, my mind had a field day. My mind still didn't realize that there is a difference between being responsible and being at fault. At one point my mother attempted suicide, I believed that was my fault as well.

I worked my way through college, often holding down several jobs at the same time. I was always trying to figure out a way to make a fast buck. I liked the thrill of thinking of myself as an outlaw. I was frequently on the wrong side of the law. There was a part of me that loved the excitement but a larger part that hated the stress. That lifestyle was about as far as I could get from who I really was. I was fortunate my schemes never worked out that well and since I never made any money at them I eventually gave up.

The further away I moved from myself, the more painful my life became. I got into a series of devastating relationships. I always wound up in pain and holding the short end of the stick. Less and less of my life was working and I was seldom happy. I felt like a victim in a bad novel. I went to a therapist for several years but I found very little relief. He wanted to put me on antidepressants. At a core level I knew that wasn't the answer. I had changed my major in college several times and didn't really know what I wanted. I had taken math courses through all the changes, so I became a math major. My senior year I took an art course and loved it, but I got my B.A. in math.

After I graduated from college I opened a stained glass studio. Even though in college I had loved art, I didn't view this as a positive step. I couldn't find a job and my mom had told me to try a stained glass kit she had in the basement. I opened my own business doing something I loved, but with an attitude of being a victim. I didn't have any other choice and my mom had made me do it. For thirteen years I did something I loved and seldom allowed myself to enjoy the experience.

Every time I started a new project or relationship I was sure that if this worked, I would be fine. I was sure the answers to my loneliness, alienation, and depression were outside of myself. The business was supposed to make me happy. I never even entertained the thought that my attitude created my happiness or my misery. It—that person, place, or thing beyond my control—was in charge of my happiness. I never thought to look inside myself for any of my answers.

I spent years building up that business, it became my whole life. The business continued to grow and I moved it into a mall in a renovated woolen mill. The store was magical. It was filled with beautiful stained glass, plants, and exotic gifts. The place was wonderful but I was always a dollar short. My mother helped me a great deal, she felt needed and that was important to me. I continued to carry a sense of guilt about her suicide attempt. I thought that I might have a chance of being happy because the business was almost making money.

I no longer had a personal life. My life was my work. I worked six days a week and designed new pieces on the seventh. I drove my employees crazy by calling them all the time because I was lonely. I felt empty. I was never happy for more then a few minutes. The only time I relaxed was when I was sick or drunk.

One Friday evening a few weeks after my birthday, I decided not to go out drinking for a change and just relax at home. I got a call from the operator telling me to call the ambulance service in my parents' home town. The only thing they would tell me was that there had been trouble. After several frantic phone calls I found out that my mother had been killed in a car accident and my father was still trapped in the car. No one was sure if he would survive. I remember screaming "oh no," then I was so busy with all the details that I never had time to feel anything. I was numb. My mother had been the only anchor I had in this world. I had made many of my choices in an attempt to please her. I thought my happiness came from pleasing her.

My father had survived but was very seriously injured. Suddenly I was an adult making life and death decisions for my father. I felt totally lost and alone. I went to sleep many nights with a bottle of vodka at my side. I knew my father would need help with his grief, so I hired a psychiatrist to take care of him. I was so good at my strong act that it took the psychiatrist over a week to ask me how I was doing. He apologized for taking so long, but I wondered why he asked at all because, of course, I was fine.

My father became romantically involved with one of his nurses while he was in the hospital. I was furious. I felt abandoned and betrayed. We began a series of lawsuits over my mother's estate. I sued him for the estate and he sued me for the cost of raising me. The lawsuits dragged on for over a year.

A year later a friend of mine introduced me to cocaine. I found the magic that allowed me to feel happy and confident again. When my mother died, I felt like a large part of me died as well. I lost my sense of drive and direction. I didn't know who I was, so I lost my will to live. When I used cocaine all that changed. I felt whole again, for a short time anyway. I felt a sense of power, I was sure I could do anything.

Behind that false sense of confidence, I made some disastrous business decisions. My shop in Vermont wasn't making money so I opened a second shop in Nantucket. My drinking and drug use was accelerating and the old feelings of emptiness were beginning to return. I was sleeping until late in the afternoon, even though mornings had always been my favorite time of day. I was a wreck physically, emotionally, and spiritually.

The doctor I was seeing in Nantucket gave me a prescription for demerol and sleeping pills. I felt like a mad chemist balancing the various drugs and alcohol, trying to feel happy but nothing was working. All my life I had prided myself on my independence, I had an image of myself as a rebel. Ironically I had always defined myself by other people's reaction to me. I had no clear sense of self. The disparity between how I felt and how I acted was beginning to get painful. I did not want to go back to Vermont, and I knew I wasn't good enough for Nantucket.

A few days after my birthday I decided I could no longer endure life. My last gamble to make my fortune and save my businesses had failed. One night I decided that enough was enough. I no longer had any hope, I knew life would always be more of the same old stuff. Although I had begun delving into spirituality and metaphysics ten years earlier, I now doubted that anything other than pain truly existed.

I vaguely remember going outside that night and talking to the stars. I asked if there was anything out there. If there was, I asked if it would please help me. I went inside and decided to take my life. I took a half bottle of sleeping pills and a half bottle of demerol on top of about a fifth of alcohol and two or three grams of cocaine. I went peacefully to sleep.

The next day some people found me. The fact that I had managed to survive was truly a miracle. I had a near death experience during which I talked to my mother. It seemed to last an eternity. She kept trying to convince me that I had to go back. She said that my work wasn't finished yet. She told me that I would be a teacher and help many. Another being of light that was there with her assured me that I would be very happy. I finally said that I would think about it. At that instant I slammed back into my body. When I woke up screaming, I was furious! One of the reasons I had tried to take my life was because I felt like a failure. Now I had even failed at death.

I wish I could say that at that point my whole life changed, but it didn't. I was still clinging to many of my limitations and old beliefs. I still felt like a victim. I didn't know that there was another way to live. I thought my mind held all the answers, now I know my answers come from my heart.

The time had come for some serious soul-searching. It was evident that my life was not working. If I was going to survive, I needed to find out who I really was and what I needed and wanted. I stopped using drugs and alcohol.

The spiritual search I had begun half-heartedly in the early 1970s now became sincere. I began meditating again. By that point in my life I was only able to experience self-pity, anger, sadness, and rage. I had spent a large part of my life feeling that I had received a raw deal; that the purpose of my life was pleasing others, which was the only measure of my value; that if I was good enough, my life would be working; that if there was a god, he was punishing me for being a bad person. I was stuck in a quagmire of remorse and self-hate.

A New Age bookstore had opened up nearby and I began reading avidly. I read stacks of books on spirituality and healing. I meditated a great deal and went for long walks in nature. Slowly, some of my feelings of hopelessness began to dissipate. I began to have hope for a happy future again. I spent the next nine months tying up loose ends. I declared bankruptcy, sold my house, said my farewells, and moved to California.

◆◆◆◆◆◆◆◆◆◆◆◆◆ ◆ ◆◆◆◆◆◆◆◆◆◆◆◆◆

FINAL NOTE

 My journey has not always been easy, but I have learned so much. Today my world is a friendly and supportive one, filled with love and happiness. My life is a miracle. There is no way I could have gotten here from where I started, yet here I sit.

In closing I would like to share with you a dream I once had. I woke up in a world where everyone had bands around their hearts. Their lives were very hard and limited. Millions of people were starving to death and the cities were filled with the homeless. They had polluted their planet. They were living from their heads and didn't respect anyone or anything. It was a lonely, painful place. Everyone seemed to have to work hard and struggle. Many of their problems didn't seem to have any solutions. As I looked into their eyes, I saw pain and hopelessness.

Their hospitals and jails were overflowing.

Then I was taken to a world where everyone was living from their hearts. Everyone was free. There was no fear or suffering. It was a world free of limitations. Everyone had all their needs and wants met. Everyone was doing what they loved. The planet was free of pollution. There were no homeless or starving children. There were no jails. It was truly Utopia.

Just imagine what it would be like to live in that world! As I began to think about the dream, I realized it *is* possible. The only difference between the two worlds was that on one, people lived from their heads and on the other they lived from their hearts. The people were the same. All the reasons I thought it couldn't work were merely beliefs I needed to release. The dream could begin with each of us. As we experience that freedom in our own lives we can share it with others. They can then share it, and so on, until we create a world free of limitations.

Every soul comes here to learn its own lessons. If enough of us learn to live from our hearts, we can show others how to do so as well and leave the need for suffering behind. I have shared this vision with others in the following mediation. I hope you enjoy it and will join me in creating Utopia in your own life.

UTOPIA MEDITATION

Allow yourself to relax totally and completely. (long pause) Find yourself floating up over your life. See your life on a line, a line of time. See your past flowing out behind you, your future in front of you. In front of you is a large bubble of light. It is pure, clear, and very inviting. You step into it. You feel totally safe, protected, and loved. You are love. You feel all your fears and limitations falling away. You feel free. (long pause)

You begin drifting back into your life, surrounded by that bubble. You begin noticing that most people have walls around their hearts. You see that all their anger, fears, and limitations come from those walls.

The bubble begins to drift in time. You find yourself in a world where everyone is free. Their hearts are open. The world is free of limitations. No one has bands around their hearts. There is no suffering, no pain. It is Utopia. Everyone is living from their hearts. (long pause) You decide you want to live in that world.

Once again you float over your time line. You gently insert that vision of the world into your life. You see yourself and everyone around you living from their hearts. It is magical. You feel free and loving. The world is so gentle. You remember that Utopia is possible. (long pause)

You step back into your time line. You know Utopia lies within you. You ask for help in creating it. You bring that reality back with you. You feel the wall around your heart melting away. You begin to live from your heart. You bring that feeling with you. Let that world begin with you.

May you walk always in the light. May your life be filled with love. May your journey be a joyous one. Come and join me in healing ourselves, each other, and our universe. Learn to love yourself and your world unconditionally.

In love and light,

Susan

DEFINITIONS

ATTENTION .... Where we direct our energy or what we choose to observe or focus our energy on.

CATCH THE ENERGY .... A phrase used to describe the ability to understand and interpret information obtained on the ethereal levels.

CHANNEL................... The ability to act as a conductor of energy.

DISCIPLINE................ The practice of taking deliberate actions. Planned actions designed to achieve a desired result.

DREAMER ....A person who accesses information from the ethereal level in the form of pictures which they then must interpret.

DUALITY ....The belief that there is a separation from the god source which creates the illusion of duality or the concepts of opposites. Examples: black and white, good and evil, right and wrong, etc.

ETHEREAL ....An energy level. In a sense it is a buffer zone between the physical and spiritual levels.

HANDLING POWER..........A person's ability to channel power. The act of channeling power to transform it; i.e. using it for healing or manifesting.

INTENTION.................What we really want to achieve by our actions.

INVOCATION ....A ceremony in which the energy of the participants and the leader is focused and directed for a specific purpose. The powers of the "gods" and the elements are also invoked for that specific goal. It is a ceremony which is not done lightly. A person might use this ceremony once in a lifetime. It is created by using a specific series of power moves. When the energy is at its peak, it is released and directed toward the goal.

MAGIC .... Power that has been transformed into a physical manifestation.

PERSONAL IMPORTANCE ..... Ego in the negative sense.

PERSONAL POWER .... The amount of power a person is able to handle or channel.

POWER..................... Energy that has been captured and is in the process of being transformed into something. The ability to take action.

POWER MOVES .... Physical movements of the body which are designed to help a person increase the amount of power he or she can handle. An example is Tai Chi.

STALKER...................A person who intuitively knows
                         blocks of information received
                         from the ethereal level. After a
                         meditation he or she returns with
                         a block of information.

STALKING ....The act of watching and pursu-
                         ing an objective such as a person,
                         place, or thing. It is usually used
                         in association with stalking power
                         and moving cautiously.